2024 MENTAL HEALTH RESOURCE GUIDE FOR NORTH CAROLINA

1st Edition

CAROLYN E. DANIELS, DMin, MEd, MDiv
LUNAR EDWARDS, JD, RN

CEHSI

2024 MENTAL HEALTH RESOURCE GUIDE FOR NORTH CAROLINA

COPYRIGHT© 2023. **All rights reserved.**
Printed in the United States of America

ISBN 979-8-218-34766-6

Editor: Daniel Pratt, MA, BA

Published by:
Carolina Eastern Health Services, Inc. (CEHSI)
Fayetteville, North Carolina
Email: cehsinc@outlook.com

PREFACE

This book will provide comprehensive resources in North Carolina concerning Mental Health. The Mental Health crisis continues to increase in the USA. Knowledge of resources is beneficial in obtaining treatment and support.

North Carolina has a hundred (100) counties. Each chapter in this book covers a county. The counties have been listed in alphabetical order. The first chapter begins with Alamance County and the last chapter is allocated to Yancey County.

Essential information about community resources is located in each county. Topics cover services for medical, substance abuse, mental health, legal, housing, transportation, food/clothing, and physical leisure activities. This guide helps to identify useful resources in local communities in the state of North Carolina.

DISCLAIMER

This resource guide is intended to provide useful information about North Carolina. Although we have listed various resources that may be helpful, we do not endorse any services or service providers listed within.

The information presented was collected from a variety of resources available via the Internet, books, and periodicals. The inclusion of any organization, program, service, or agency does not imply a recommendation nor does exclusion imply disapproval. Individuals should rely on their own needs, opinions, and perceptions in choosing which services to access.

CONTENTS

PREFACE		i
DISCLAIMER		iii
FORWARD		ix
ACKNOWLEDGMENTS		xi
Chapter 1.	Alamance County	1
Chapter 2.	Alexander County	4
Chapter 3.	Allegheny County	7
Chapter 4.	Anson County	9
Chapter 5.	Ashe County	11
Chapter 6.	Avery County	13
Chapter 7.	Beaufort County	15
Chapter 8.	Bertie County	17
Chapter 9.	Bladen County	19
Chapter 10.	Brunswick County	21
Chapter 11.	Buncombe County	24
Chapter 12.	Burke County	28
Chapter 13.	Cabarrus County	30
Chapter 14.	Caldwell County	33
Chapter 15.	Camden County	37
Chapter 16.	Carteret County	40
Chapter 17.	Caswell County	44
Chapter 18.	Catawba County	47
Chapter 19.	Chatham County	51
Chapter 20.	Cherokee County	54

Chapter 21.	Chowan County	56
Chapter 22.	Clay County	59
Chapter 23.	Cleveland County	61
Chapter 24.	Columbus County	65
Chapter 25.	Craven County	69
Chapter 26.	Cumberland County	72
Chapter 27.	Currituck County	76
Chapter 28.	Dare County	79
Chapter 29.	Davidson County	82
Chapter 30.	Davie County	84
Chapter 31.	Duplin County	86
Chapter 32.	Durham County	89
Chapter 33.	Edgecombe County	92
Chapter 34.	Forsyth County	96
Chapter 35.	Franklin County	99
Chapter 36.	Gaston County	102
Chapter 37.	Gates County	105
Chapter 38.	Graham County	108
Chapter 39.	Granville County	110
Chapter 40.	Greene County	112
Chapter 41.	Guilford County	115
Chapter 42.	Halifax County	118
Chapter 43.	Harnett County	120
Chapter 44.	Haywood County	122
Chapter 45.	Henderson County	124
Chapter 46.	Hertford County	126
Chapter 47.	Hoke County	129
Chapter 48.	Hyde County	132
Chapter 49.	Iredell County	135

Chapter 50.	Jackson County	138
Chapter 51.	Johnston County	140
Chapter 52.	Jones County	144
Chapter 53.	Lee County	147
Chapter 54.	Lenoir County	149
Chapter 55.	Lincoln County	152
Chapter 56.	Macon County	155
Chapter 57.	Madison County	157
Chapter 58.	Martin County	159
Chapter 59.	McDowell County	162
Chapter 60.	Mecklenburg County	165
Chapter 61.	Mitchell County	169
Chapter 62.	Montgomery County	172
Chapter 63.	Moore County	174
Chapter 64.	Nash County	176
Chapter 65.	New Hanover County	179
Chapter 66.	Northampton County	182
Chapter 67.	Onslow County	185
Chapter 68.	Orange County	188
Chapter 69.	Pamlico County	191
Chapter 70.	Pasquotank County	194
Chapter 71.	Pender County	197
Chapter 72.	Perquimans County	200
Chapter 73.	Person County	203
Chapter 74.	Pitt County	205
Chapter 75.	Polk County	209
Chapter 76.	Randolph County	211
Chapter 77.	Richmond County	214
Chapter 78.	Robeson County	217

Chapter 79.	Rockingham County	221
Chapter 80.	Rowan County	223
Chapter 81.	Rutherford County	226
Chapter 82.	Sampson County	230
Chapter 83.	Scotland County	233
Chapter 84.	Stanly County	236
Chapter 85.	Stokes County	239
Chapter 86.	Surry County	241
Chapter 87.	Swain County	243
Chapter 88.	Transylvania County	245
Chapter 89.	Tyrrell County	247
Chapter 90.	Union County	250
Chapter 91.	Vance County	252
Chapter 92.	Wake County	255
Chapter 93.	Warren County	258
Chapter 94.	Washington County	261
Chapter 95.	Watauga County	264
Chapter 96.	Wayne County	266
Chapter 97.	Wilkes County	270
Chapter 98.	Wilson County	272
Chapter 99.	Yadkin County	275
Chapter 100.	Yancey County	278
Appendix 1.	MAP OF NORTH CAROLINA, USA (COUNTIES)	280

FORWARD

It is a pleasure to write the forward for this book. I was honored for the opportunity to be a co-author of this project. This was a collaboration of many caring souls, long hours, and years of dedication. I hope that it will be useful and serve as a beacon of light to individuals and their loved ones who need support and services.

By

Dr. Carolyn E. Daniels

ACKNOWLEDGMENTS

We wish to thank our editor, Mr. Daniel Pratt, for his energy, enthusiasm, and contributions to this book.

We were truly blessed to have excellent reviewers work with us on this edition.

Also, we want to express our genuine gratitude to our families for their unwavering love and support throughout this project. Most importantly, we thank God for the strength and courage provided to us during the COVID-19 epidemic, loss of family members, and personal struggles.

CHAPTER 1

Alamance County

1. **Mental Health and Crisis Services**
Alamance- Caswell Mental Health Center
319 N. Graham-Hopedale Rd., Suite A
Burlington, NC 27217
336-431-4200 or 336-513-4444

2. **Substance Abuse Services**
RHA Health Services
2732 Anne Elizabeth Drive
Burlington, NC 27215
336-229-5905

3. **Clothing/ Food Assistance/ Financial Services**
Alamance County Meals on Wheels
411 W. 5th St., Suite A
Burlington, NC 27215
336-228-8815

Alamance Rescue Mission
1519 N. Mebane Street
Burlington, NC 27217
336-228-0782 or 336-229-6995

The Healing Station Food Pantry
802 Chapel Hill Rd.
Burlington, North Carolina
336-639-1103

The Salvation Army
812 N. Anthony St.
Burlington, NC 27217
336-227-4462 or 336-227-5529

4. **Housing and Shelters**
Alamance Rescue Mission
129 W. Holt St.
Burlington, North Carolina
336-228-0782

Burlington Housing Authority
133 N. Ireland St.
Burlington, NC 27217
336-226-8421

Graham Housing Authority
109 E. Hill St.
Graham, NC 27253
336-229-7041

The Salvation Army
426 N. Church St.
Burlington, North Carolina
336-227-1011

5. **Transportation**
Alamance
County Transportation
Authority (ACTA)
1946-C Martin Street
Burlington, NC 27217
336-222-0565

6. **Medical Services**
Alamance County
Health Department
319 N. Graham-Hopedale
Road, #B
Burlington, NC 27217
336-227-0101 or 336-570-6413

7. **Medication
Assistance Program**
Alamance County Department
of Social Services
319-C North Graham-
Hopedale Road
Burlington, NC 27217
336-570-6532

Alamance County Prescription
Drug Card
336-228-1312

Open Door Clinic
319-E North Graham-
Hopedale Road
Burlington, NC 27217
336-570-9800

8. **Employment/ Vocational
Rehab/ Education**
NC Works Career Center
2640 Columbine Lane
Burlington, NC 27215
336-570-6800

Vocational Rehabilitation
2615 Alamance Rd.
Burlington, NC 27215
336-570-6855

9. **Legal Services**
Legal Aid of
NC-Guilford County
122 N. Elm St.
Greensboro, NC 27401
336-227-0148

Legal Aid of
NC-Chatham County
959 East St., Suite A&B
Pittsboro, North Carolina
919-542-0475

10. **Recreational/ Leisure**
Alamance County
Visitors Bureau
200 S. Main St.
Burlington, NC 27215
336-570-1444

11. **Special Populations**
Family Abuse Services
(Domestic Violence)
1950 Martin St.
Burlington, NC 27217
336-226-5982 or (Crisis Line)
336-226-5985

HIV/AIDS Support
336-538-8111
JRK Senior Activity Center
1535 S. Mebane St.
Burlington, NC 27215
336-222-5030

Services for Blind
336-896-2227

Services for Deaf
336-273-9692

Veterans Services of
Alamance County
201 W. Elm St.
Graham, NC 27253
336-570-6783

Veterans Service Office
217 College St.
Graham, North Carolina
336-221-8029

CHAPTER 2

Alexander County

1. **Mental Health and Crisis Services**
Family Guidance Center-
Catawba County
17 US Highway 70, SE
Hickory, NC 28602
828-322-1400

2. **Substance Abuse Services**
Smokey Mountain Center-
Jackson County
44 Bonnie Ln.
Sylva, North Carolina
828-586-5501

3. **Clothing/ Food Assistance/ Financial Services**
Alexander County Good
Samaritan Food Pantry
9369 NC-127
Hickory, NC 28601
828-495-8251

CCC (Food)
215 5th Ave., SW
Taylorsville, NC 28681
828-632-0022

Salvation Army Thrift Store
(Clothing)
226 Westgate Dr.
Taylorsville, NC 28681
828-636-3882

4. **Housing and Shelters**
Safe Shelter
(Domestic Violence)
828-228-1787

Shelter of Hope/The Salvation
Army- Catawba County
760 3rd Avenue Place, SE
Hickory, NC 28602
828-322-8061

Western Piedmont COG
(Section 8)-Catawba County
P.O. Box 9026
Hickory, North Carolina
828-322-9191

5. **Transportation**
Greenway
Public Transportation/
Western Piedmont Regional
Transit Authority
1515 4th St., SW
Conover, NC 28613
828-465-7634

6. **Medical Services**
Alexander County
Public Health
338 1st Ave., SW
Taylorsville, NC 28681
828-632-9704

Alexander County
Dental Clinic
338 1st Ave., SW
Taylorsville, NC 28681
828-632-9704

7. **Medication
Assistance Program**
Alexander County Department
of Social Services
604 7th St., SW
Taylorsville, NC 28681
828-632-1080

Good Rx
855-268-2822

Needy Meds
800-503-6897

Rx Outreach
P.O. Box 66536
St. Louis, MO 63166
888-796-1234

8. **Employment/ Vocational
Rehab/ Education**
Employment Service
Commission (ESC)
604 7th St., SW
Taylorsville, NC 28681
828-632-4631

9. **Legal Services**
Legal Aid-Burke County
211 E. Union St.
Morganton, NC 28655
828-219-5262, 828-437-8280,
or 800-849-5195

10. **Recreational/ Leisure**
Alexander County
Visitor Center
151 W. Main Ave.
Taylorsville, NC 28681
828-632-8141

Bethlehem Park
187 Bethlehem Park Lane
Taylorsville, NC 28681

Parks and Recreation
151 W. Main St., Suite 1
Taylorsville, NC 28681
828-632-1104

11. **Special Populations**
Alexander County Information
2-1-1
211 or 828-632-1161 or
888-892-1162

Alexander County
Senior Center
730 7th St., SW
Taylorsville, NC 28681
828-632-1717

Domestic Violence Center
P.O. Box 652
Taylorsville, North Carolina
828-635-8850/ Crisis Line
– 828-635-8881

Senior Center
Stony Point United Methodist
311 Ruritan Park Road
Stony Point, NC 28678
828-632-1717

Veterans Services
621 Liledoun Road
Taylorsville, NC 28681
828-632-5411

CHAPTER 3

Allegheny County

1. **Mental Health and Crisis Services**
New River Behavioral Healthcare, LME-Watauga County
895 State Farm Road, Suite 508
Boone, North Carolina 28607
336-372-4095

2. **Substance Abuse Services**
DayMark Recovery Services
1650 Highway 18 S.
Sparta, NC 28675
336-372-2722

3. **Clothing/ Food Assistance/ Financial Services**
Allegheny Memorial Hospital-Thrift Store
372 US-21
Roaring Gap, NC 28668
336-363-3194

Solid Rock Food Closet
71 Womble St.
Sparta, NC 28675
336-372-6560

The Salvation Army-Mount Airy
336-786-4075

4. **Housing and Shelters**
Hospitality House (Shelter)
338 Brook Hollow Rd.
Boone, NC 28607
828-264-1237

Northwestern Regional Housing-Wilkes County
215 W. South St.
Wilkesboro, NC 28697
336-667-8979

5. **Transportation**
Allegheny in Motion
90 S. Main St.
Sparta, NC 28675
336-372-8747

6. **Medical Services**
Allegheny County Health Department
157 Health Services Rd.
Sparta, NC 28675
336-372-5641

Medi Home Health & Hospice
403 S. Main St., #101
Sparta, NC 28675
336-372-8018

7. **Medication
Assistance Program**
Allegheny County Department
of Social Services
182 Doctors St.
Sparta, NC 28675
336-372-2411

Allegheny CARES
Medication Assistance
25 Womble St.
Sparta, NC 28675
336-372-5959

8. **Employment/ Vocational
Rehab/ Education**
NC Works Career Center
115 Atwood St.
Sparta, NC 28675
336-372-9675

Vocational Rehabilitation-
Wilkes County
318 Wilkesboro Ave., North
North Wilkesboro, NC 28659
336-667-1205

9. **Legal Services**
Legal Aid of NC
171 Grand Blvd.
Boone, NC 28607
828-355-4890 or 800-849-5666

10. **Recreational/ Leisure**
Allegheny County
Visitor Center
58 S. Main St.
Sparta, NC 28675
336-372-5473

11. **Special Populations**
Allegheny Senior Center
336-372-7677

Allegheny Senior Services
30 Wellness Way
Sparta, NC 28675
336-372-46408

D.A.N.A. Services
(Domestic Violence)
P.O. Box 1643
Sparta, North Carolina
336-372-2846/Crisis Line
– 336-372-3262

Veterans Service Officer
County Office Building
348 S. Main St.
Sparta, NC 28675
336-372-4850

CHAPTER 4

Anson County

1. **Mental Health and Crisis Services**
Moore County
Sandhills Center
P.O. Box 9
West End, North Carolina
910-673-9111

2. **Substance Abuse Services**
AA-Monroe
704-312-1532

DayMark Recovery Services
704 Old Lilesville Rd.
Wadesboro, NC 28170
704-694-6588

3. **Clothing/ Food Assistance/ Financial Services**
Anson Crisis Ministry
117 N. Rutherford St.
Wadesboro, NC 28170
704-694-2445

Harvest Ministries-Food
Distribution Center
1134 E. Caswell Street
Wadesboro, NC 28170
704-695-2879

Feed My Lambs, Inc.
2290 US-74 W.
Wadesboro, NC 28170
704-695-1820

4. **Housing and Shelters**
Wadesboro Housing Authority
200 W. Short Plaza
Wadesboro, NC 28170
704-694-4852

5. **Transportation**
Anson County Transportation
Services (ACTS)
575 US Highway 52 S.
Wadesboro, NC 28170
704-694-2596

6. **Medical Services**
Anson County
Health Department
110 Ashe St.
Wadesboro, NC 28170
704-694-5188

Atrium Health-Anson
2301 US Highway 74 W.
Wadesboro, NC 28170
704-994-4500

7. **Medication
Assistance Program**
Anson County Department of
Social Services
118 N. Washington St.
Wadesboro, NC 28170
704-694-9351

8. **Employment/ Vocational
Rehab/ Education**
NC Vocational Rehabilitation-
Richmond County
1793 E. Broad Ave.
Rockingham, NC 28379
910-997-9230

NC Works Career Center
514 N. Washington St.
Wadesboro, NC 28170
704-272-5479 or 704-272-5475

9. **Legal Services**
Legal Aid of Concord-
Cabarrus County
785 Davidson Dr.
Concord, North Carolina
704-786-4145 or 800-849-8009

Legal Aid of
NC-Chatham County
117 E. Salisbury St.
Pittsboro, NC 27312
919-542-0475 or 800-672-5834

10. **Recreational/ Leisure**
Anson County Visitors Center
114 W. Wade St.
Wadesboro, NC 28170
704-694-4181

11. **Special Populations**
Anson County DV Coalition
(Domestic Violence)
304 E. Wade St.
Wadesboro, NC 28170
704-694-4499

Anson County Veteran
Service Department
575 US Highway 52 S.
Wadesboro, NC 28170
704-465-0086

Grace Senior Center
199 Highway 742, South
Wadesboro, NC 28170
704-694-6431

CHAPTER 5

Ashe County

1. ***Mental Health and Crisis Services***
New River Behavioral Healthcare, LME-Watauga County
895 State Farm Road, Suite 508
Boone, North Carolina 28607
828-264-9007

Smokey Mountain Center, LME-Jackson County
44 Bonnie Ln.
Sylva, NC 28779
828-486-5501

2. ***Substance Abuse Services***
DayMark Recovery Services
101 Colvard St.
Jefferson, NC 28640
336-246-4542

3. ***Clothing/ Food Assistance/ Financial Services***
Goodwill (Clothing)
1291 Mount Jefferson Rd.
West Jefferson, NC 28694
336-219-0244

Ashe Outreach (Food Pantry)
336-385-1314

Ashe Really Cares (Food/Clothing)
204 Beaver Creek School Rd.
West Jefferson, NC 28694
336-846-5631

Ashe County Sharing Center Food Pantry
115 Colvard St.
Jefferson, NC 28640
336-846-7109

4. ***Housing and Shelters***
A Safe Home For Everyone (Shelter)
1622 Highway 221 N.
Jefferson, NC 28640
336-982-8851

Hospitality House (Shelter)-Watauga County
302 King St.
Boone, North Carolina
828-264-1237

5. **Transportation**
Ashe County
Transportation Authority
895 Ray Taylor Rd.
West Jefferson, NC 28694
336-846-2000

6. **Medical Services**
Appalachian District
Health Department
413 McConnell Street
Jefferson, NC 28640
336-246-9449

7. **Medication
Assistance Program**
Ashe County Department of
Social Services
150 Governments Cir.,
Suite 1400
Jefferson, NC 28640
336-846-5179

8. **Employment/ Vocational
Rehab/ Education**
NC Works
103 Calls St., Extension
Wilkesboro, NC 28697
336-838-5164

Vocational Rehabilitation
245 Winkler's Creek Road
Boone, NC 28607
828-265-5396

9. **Legal Services**
Legal Aid-Watauga County
171 Grand Blvd.
Boone, North Carolina
828-264-5640 or 800-849-5666

10. **Recreational/Leisure**
Ashe County Chamber &
Visitor Center
1 N. Jefferson Ave.
West Jefferson, NC 28694
336-846-9550

11. **Special Populations**
SAFE House
(Domestic Violence)
336-982-4588/Crisis Line
336-219-2600

Veterans Services
150 Government Cir.
Jefferson, NC 28640
336-846-5575

CHAPTER 6

Avery County

1. **Mental Health and Crisis Services**
New River Behavioral Healthcare, LME-Watauga County
895 State Farm Road, Suite 508
Boone, NC 28607
828-264-9007

2. **Substance Abuse Services**
DayMark Recovery Services-Avery Center
360 Beech St.
Newland, NC 28657
828-733-5889

3. **Clothing/ Food Assistance/ Financial Services**
Feeding Avery Families
130 Montezuma St.
Newland, NC 28657
828-260-6043

Hospitality House of Boone Area, Inc.-Watauga County
337 Brook Hollow Rd.
Boone, NC 28607
828-264-1237

RAMS Rack-Emergency Food Pantry
147 New Vale Rd.
Newland, NC 28657
828-733-4305 or 828-733-5127

WIC Program
828-733-6052

4. **Housing and Shelters**
Hospitality House (Shelter)
302 King St.
Boone, North Carolina
828-264-1237

North Western Regional Housing Authority
253 Elk Park School Rd.
Elk Park, North Carolina
828-733-1546

5. **Transportation**
Avery County Transportation
34 Pershing St.
Newland, NC 28657
828-733-0005

6. **Medical Services**
Appalachian
Regional Healthcare
434 Hospital Dr.
Newland, North Carolina
828-733-7000

Avery County
Health Department
545 Schultz Cir.
Newland, NC 28657
828-733-6031

7. **Medication
Assistance Program**
Avery County Department of
Social Services
175 Linville St.
Newland, NC 28657
828-733-8230

8. **Employment/ Vocational
Rehab/ Education**
Job Corps-Transylvania County
98 Schenck Drive
Pisgah Forest, NC 28768
828-862-6100

NC Works Career Center
785 Cranberry St.
Newland, NC 28657
828-766-1385

Vocational Rehabilitation
815 Pineola St.
Newland, NC 28657
828-733-9345

9. **Legal Services**
Legal Aid-Watauga County
171 Grand Blvd.
Boone, NC 28607
828-264-5640, 866-219-5262,
or 800-849-5666

10. **Recreational/ Leisure**
Visitor Center- (Intersection of
NC 105 & NC 184)
4501 Tyncastle Hwy., Unit 2
Banner Elk, NC 28604
828-898-5605 or 800-972-2183

11. **Special Populations**
ACADA Home Inc.
(Domestic Violence)
Crisis Line-828-733-3512

Avery County Senior Center
165 Schultz Cir.
Newland, NC 28657
828-733-8220

Avery County Veterans
Service Office
175 Linville St.
Newland, NC 28657
828-733-8211

OASIS, Inc.
(Domestic Violence)
828-262-5035

CHAPTER 7

Beaufort County

1. **Mental Health and Crisis Services**
East Carolina Behavioral
Health, ,LME
252-329-1810

   ECU Health/Behavioral Health
1308 Highland Dr.
Washington, NC 27889
252-946-3666

   Integrated Family Services
1308 Highland Dr.
Washington, NC 27889
866-437-1821

2. **Substance Abuse Services**
Family Wellness Center
1235 Highland Dr.
Washington, NC 27889
252-215-9011

   PORT Health
1379 Colwell Farm Rd.
Washington, NC 27889

3. **Clothing/ Food Assistance/ Financial Services**
Martha's Pantry
1014 US-264 Bypass
Belhaven, NC 27810
252-943-2124

   Salvation Army
112 E. 7th St.
Washington, North Carolina
252-946-2523

4. **Housing and Shelters**
Eagle's Wings
932 W. 3rd St.
Washington, NC 27889
752-975-1138

   Open Door Community Shelter
(Women)
252-833-8492

   Washington Housing Authority
809 Pennsylvania Ave.
Washington, NC 27889
252-946-0061

Zion Shelter-Soup Kitchen (Men)
114 E. Martin Luther King Junior Drive
Washington, NC 27889
252-975-1978

5. **Transportation**
Beaufort Area Transit System- (B.A.T.S.)
1537 W. 5th St.
Washington, NC 27889
252-946-5778

6. **Medical Services**
Beaufort County Health Department
1436 Highland Dr.
Washington, North Carolina
252-946-1902

7. **Medication Assistance Program**
Beaufort County Department of Social Services
632 W. 5th St.
Washington, NC 27889
252-975-5500

8. **Employment/ Vocational Rehab/ Education**
NC Works
1502 N. Market St., Suite B
Washington, NC 27889

Vocational Rehabilitation
953 Washington St.
Washington, NC 27889
252-623-5430

9. **Legal Services**
Legal Aid of NC- Pitt County
301 Evans St., Suite 102
Greenville, NC 27858
252-758-0113 or 866-219-5262

NC Lawyer Referral Service
800-662-7407

10. **Recreational/ Leisure**
Little Washington Visitors Center
102 Stewart Pkwy.
Washington, NC 27889
800-546-0162

11. **Special Populations**
Beaufort County Veterans Services
1308 Highland Dr., #104
Washington, NC 27889
252-946-8016

Mobile Crisis Team
866-437-1821

Suicide Prevention
"988"

Washington Senior Resource Center
310 W. Main St.
Washington, NC 27889
252-975-9368

CHAPTER 8

Bertie County

1. **Mental Health and Crisis Services**
East Carolina Behavioral
Health, LME- Hertford County
144 Community College Rd.
Ahoskie, North Carolina
252-332-4137

2. **Substance Abuse Services**
Windsor Community
Health Center
104 Rhodes Ave.
Windsor, NC 27983
252-794-1835 x 226

3. **Clothing/ Food Assistance/ Financial Services**
Askewville Community
Food Pantry
102 E. Askewville Street
Windsor, NC 27983
252-325-3467

Good Shepherd Food Pantry
1008 N. King St.
Windsor, NC 27983
252-370-0324

Salvation Army-
Pasquotank County
602 N. Hughes Blvd.
Elizabeth City, North Carolina
252-338-4129

Meals on Wheels
252-312-6213

4. **Housing and Shelters**
Bertie-Martin-Beaufort Shelter
Home (Boys)
2295 Main St.
Jamesville, North Carolina
252-792-1863

Bertie-Martin-Beaufort Shelter
Home (Girls)-Martin County
1111 NaiRad Ln.
Williamston, North Carolina
252-792-8357

Rowan-Chowan S.A.F.E.-
Hertford County
P.O. Box 98
Ahoskie, NC 27910
252-332-1933

5. **Transportation**
All Hearts Transportation
Services-Martin County
138 W. Main St.
Williamston, North Carolina
252-217-1922

Transportation Department
1740 Prison Camp Rd.
Williamston, North Carolina
252-794-4356

6. **Medical Services**
Bertie County
Health Department
102 Rhodes Ave.
Windsor, NC 27983
252-794-5322

7. **Medication Assistance Program**
Bertie County Department of
Social Services
110 Jasper Bazemore Ave.
Windsor, NC 27983
252-794-5320

8. **Employment/ Vocational Rehab/ Education**
Job Link Center
1001 S. King St.
Windsor, NC 27983
252-794-5616

Vocational Rehabilitation-
Pasquotank County
401 S. Griffin St.
Elizabeth City, NC 27909
252-331-4768

9. **Legal Services**
Legal Services of Coastal
Plains- Hertford County
610 E. Church St., East
Ahoskie, NC 27910
252-332-5124

10. **Recreational/ Leisure**
Bertie County Visitors Center
121 E. Granville St.
Windsor, NC 27983
252-794-4277

11. **Special Populations**
Senior Center
103 W. School St.
Windsor, North Carolina
252-794-5315

Veteran Services
106 Dundee St.
Windsor, North Carolina
252-794-5304

CHAPTER 9

Bladen County

1. **Mental Health and Crisis Services**
Bladen County Mental Health
P.O. Box 1176
Elizabethtown, NC 28337
910-862-6870

CommWell Health
877-935-5255

Coastal SE United Care
910-863-4003

Eastpointe Mental Health
800-913-6109

2. **Substance Abuse Services**
Coastal Horizons
209 Peanut Plant Rd.
Elizabethtown, NC 28337
910-640-3849 or 910-524-8183

RHA Health Services
106 4th St.
Bladenboro, North Carolina
910-613-0900 or 800-848-0180

The Carter Clinic
1104 W. Broad Street
Elizabethtown, North Carolina
910-991-3070

3. **Clothing/ Food Assistance/ Financial Services**
American Red Cross
800-HELP NOW

Baldwin Branch MBC-
Food Pantry
4047 NC 242 Highway, South
Elizabethtown, North Carolina
910-645-2396

Bladen Crisis Food Pantry
208 S. Morehead St.
Elizabethtown, NC 28337
910-879-1032

4. **Housing and Shelters**
Bladenboro Housing Authority
117 Main St.
Bladenboro, North Carolina
910-863-4919

Families First (Shelter)
910-642-5996

5. **Transportation**
Bladen Area Rural
Transportation System
(BARTS)
608 McLeod St.
Elizabethtown, NC 28337
910-862-6930

6. **Medical Services**
Bladen County Free Clinic
Highway 87 W.
Council, NC 28434
910-669-3272

Bladen County
Health Department
300 Mercer Mill Road
Elizabethtown, NC 28337
910-862-6900

7. **Medication
Assistance Program**
Bladen County Department of
Social Services
208 McKay St.
Elizabethtown, NC 28337
910-862-6800

8. **Employment/ Vocational
Rehab/ Education**
Bladen County JobLink
Career Center
401 Mercer Mill Rd.
Elizabethtown, NC 28337
910-862-3255

Department of
Vocational Rehabilitation
2948 W. Broad Street
Elizabethtown, NC 28337
910-872-5570 or 910-872-5569

9. **Legal Services**
NC Legal Aide of Wilmington
201 N. Front St., Suite 1002
Wilmington, NC 28401
910-763-6207

10. **Recreational/ Leisure**
Elizabethtown
Information Center
207 E. Broad Street, Suite B
Elizabethtown, NC 28337
910-862-4368

11. **Special Populations**
Bladen County Veterans
Service Office
301 Cypress St.
Elizabethtown, NC 28337
910-862-6950

Family Violence Center
(Domestic Violence)
Crisis Line – 910-641-0444

Senior Center
109 Elm St.
Bladenboro, NC 28320
910-862-6930

Senior Center
608 McLeod St.
Elizabethtown, NC 28337
910-872-6338

CHAPTER 10

Brunswick County

1. **Mental Health and Crisis Services**
Brunswick County DSS-MH / SA
25 Courthouse Dr.
Bolivia, NC 28422
910-253-2250

Novant Health
Psychiatric Medicine
512 Village Rd., Suite 104
Shallotte, NC 28470
910-721-4200

2. **Substance Abuse Services**
Coastal Horizons Center Inc.
120 Coastal Horizons Dr.
Shallotte, NC 28470
910-754-4515

3. **Clothing/ Food Assistance/ Financial Services**
Brunswick Family
Assistance Agency
4600 Main St.
Shallotte, NC 27470
910-754-4766

WIC Program
1492 Village Rd., NE
Leland, NC 28451
910-253-2878

4. **Housing and Shelters**
Brunswick County
Housing Authority
60 Government Center Dr., NE
Bolivia, NC 28422
910-253-2222

Hope Harbor Home (Females)
1053 Ocean Hwy., West
Bolivia, NC 28422
910-253-2222

Providence Home Family
Emergency Shelter (Teens)
5310 Dosher Cutoff
Southpoint, NC 28461
910-253-2670

5. **Transportation**
Brunswick Transit System, Inc.
5040 Main St.
Shallotte, NC 28470
910-253-7800

6. **Medical Services**
Brunswick County
Health Department
25 Courthouse Dr., Building A
Bolivia, NC 28422
910-253-2250 or 888-428-4429

New Hope Clinic
201 W. Boiling Spring Lake Rd.
Boiling Spring Lake, NC 28461
910-845-5333

7. **Medication Assistance Program**
Brunswick County Department
of Social Services
60 Government Center Dr., NE
Bolivia, North Carolina
910-253-2077

Good Rx
855-268-2822

Needy Meds
800-503-6897

Rx Outreach
P.O. Box 66536
St. Louis, MO 63166
888-796-1234

8. **Employment/ Vocational Rehab/ Education**
Brunswick Career Center
5300 Main St., #7
Shallotte, NC 28470
910-754-6120

Vocational
Rehabilitation Services
25 Courthouse Dr.
Bolivia, NC 28422
910-253-2223

9. **Legal Services**
Legal Aid of NC
201 N. Front St.
Wilmington, North Carolina
910-763-6207

10. **Recreational/ Leisure**
Brunswick County
Visitors Center
394 Whiteville Rd., NW
Shallotte, NC 28470
910-754-2505

Oak Island Recreation Center
300 E. Oak Island Dr.
Oak Island, North Carolina
910-278-5018

11. **Special Populations**
Brunswick Senior Resources
35 Courthouse Dr., NE
Building D
Bolivia, NC 28422
910-253-2199

National Domestic
Violence Hotline
800-799-7233

National Suicide
Prevention Line
800-273-8255

Shallotte Senior Citizens Center
5040 Main St.
Shallotte, NC 28470
910-754-2300

Southport Senior
Citizens Center
209 N. Atlantic Ave.
Southport, NC 28461
910-754-2300

Veterans Crisis Hotline
800-273-8255
Veteran's Services
10 Referendum Dr.
Building F
Bolivia, North Carolina
910-251-5710

CHAPTER 11

Buncombe County

1. **Mental Health and Crisis Services**
PATH at Homeward Bound
19 N. Ann Street
Asheville, North Carolina
828-252-8883

Smokey Mountain Center/
Western Highlands, LME
356 Biltmore Ave.
Asheville, North Carolina
800-849-6127 or 828-225-2800

RHA Behavioral
Health Services
90 Ashland Ave.
Asheville, North Carolina
828-254-2700

RHA Health Services (Mobile
Crisis Team)
888-573-1006

2. **Substance Abuse Services**
Alcoholics Anonymous
70 Woodfin Place, Suite 206
Asheville, North Carolina
828-254-8539

Blue Ridge Center-
Mental Health/Substance
Abuse Program
Buncombe County,
North Carolina
828-258-3500

Crest View Recovery Center
90 Ashland Ave.
Asheville, NC 28801
855-745-6448

Insight Recovery Center
2123 Hendersonville Rd.
Arden, NC 28704
828-471-4650

Next Step Recovery
900 Hendersonville Rd.,
Suite 203
Asheville, NC 28803
828-970-1501

Oasis Recovery Center
191 Charlotte St.
Asheville, NC 28801
828-373-8228

SMART Recovery
(Support Group)
871 Merrimon Ave.
Asheville, North Carolina
828-407-0460

3. *Clothing/ Food Assistance/
Financial Services*
ABCCM
1543 Patton Ave.
Asheville, North Carolina
828-259-5300

Beloved Street Pantries
(Food Pantry)
828-571-0766

Salvation Army
204 Haywood Street
Asheville, North Carolina
252-253-4720

Western Carolina
Rescue Ministries
225 Patton Ave.

Asheville, North Carolina
828-254-0471

WIC Clinic
282-771-5436

4. *Housing and Shelters*
ABCCM- Men's Shelter
207 Coxe Ave.
Asheville, North Carolina
828-259-5333

ABCCM- Women's Shelter
30 Cumberland Ave.
Asheville, North Carolina
828-398-6980

AHOPE Day Center (Shelter)
222 S. French Broad Avenue
Asheville, North Carolina
828-252-8883

Asheville Housing Authority
165 S. French Broad Ave.
Asheville, North Carolina
828-258-1222

French Broad (Shelter)
13 Park Ave.
Asheville, NC 28803
828-254-5346

Oxford House (Men
in Recovery)
16 Michigan Ave.
Asheville, North Carolina
828-350-1745

Oxford House (Women
in Recovery)
72 Wyoming Rd.
Asheville, North Carolina
828-254-1001

Western Carolina Rescue
Mission (Men)
225 Patton Ave.
Asheville, North Carolina
828-254-0471

5. *Transportation*
Asheville Transit Authority
(ART)
360 W. Haywood St.
Asheville, North Carolina
252-253-5691

Mountain Mobility
828-250-6750
RIDE Program
828-251-7463

6. **Medical Services**
Buncombe County
Health Department
3 S. Woodfin St.
Asheville, NC 28801
828-250-5000 or 828-250-5214

Veteran Hospital
1100 Tunnel Rd.
Asheville, North Carolina
828-298-7911

Western NC Community
Health Services (WNCCHS)
257 Biltmore Ave.
Asheville, North Carolina
828-285-0622

7. **Medication Assistance Program**
Buncombe County Department
of Social Services
3 S. Woodfin St.
Asheville, NC 28801
828-250-5500

GoodRx
855-268-2822

WNCAP (HIV/AIDS)
554 Fairview Road
Asheville, North Carolina
828-252-7489

8. **Employment/ Vocational Rehab/ Education**
Division of
Vocational Rehabilitation
8 Barbetta Dr.
Asheville, NC 28806
252-670-3377

Goodwill Industries
1616 Patton Ave.
Asheville, North Carolina
252-298-9023

Mountain Area JobLink Center
40 Coxe Ave.
Suite G 040
Asheville, NC 28802
828-250-4761

NC Works Career Center/ESC
48 Grove St.
Asheville, NC 28801
828-251-6200

9. **Legal Services**
Legal Aid
184 E. Chestnut Ave.
Asheville, North Carolina
828-239-2980

Legal Aid of North Carolina
547 Haywood Road
Asheville, North Carolina
866-219-5262

Pisgah Legal Aid
89 Montford Ave.
Asheville, North Carolina
828-253-0406

10. *Recreational/Leisure*

Asheville Visitor Center
36 Montford Avenue
Asheville, NC 28801
828-258-6129

Black Mountain-Swannanoa
Chamber of Commerce
201 E. State Street
Black Mountain, NC 28711
828-258-6104

Blue Ridge Visitor Center
195 Hemphill Knob Rd.
Asheville, NC 28803
828-298-5330

11. *Special Populations*

ABCCM (Veteran Assistance)
828-398-6609

First Call for HELP
(Referral Service)
828-252-4357

Helpmate (Domestic Violence)
68 Grove St., Suite C
Asheville, North Carolina
828-254-2968

Interface (Domestic
Violence Program)
828-252-1155

Senior Center
36 Grove St.
Asheville, NC 28801
828-350-2062

Veterans Services
1 Dundee Street
Asheville, North Carolina
828-771-6979

CHAPTER 12

Burke County

1. **Mental Health and Crisis Services**
Broughton Hospital
1000 S. Sterling St.
Morganton, NC 28655
828-433-2111

   Foothills Area Authority, LME
305 S. King St.
Morganton, North Carolina
828-438-6230

2. **Substance Abuse Services**
Frye Regional Medical Center
420 N. Center St.
Hickory, NC 28601
828-315-5000

3. **Clothing/ Food Assistance/ Financial Services**
Burke United
Christian Ministries
305 W. Union St.
Morganton, North Carolina
828-433-8075

Food and Nutrition Services/
SNAP
828-764-9600

The Outreach Center
510 Fleming Dr.
Morganton, NC 28655
828-439-8300

WIC Program
828-764-9150

4. **Housing and Shelters**
Morganton Housing Authority
644 1st St.
Morganton, NC 28655
828-437-9101

The Meeting Place
(Shelter-Men)
701 E. Meeting St.
Morganton, North Carolina
828-437-6268

Valdese Housing Authority
1402 Lydia Ave., NW
Valdese, NC 28690
828-874-0098

5. **Transportation**
   Western Piedmont Regional
   Transportation Authority
   1515 4th Street, SW
   Conover, NC 28613
   828-465-7634

6. **Medical Services**
   Burke County
   Health Department
   700 E. Parker Rd.
   Morganton, NC 28655
   828-764-9150

   Good Samaritan Clinic
   500 E. Parker Rd.
   Morganton, NC 28655
   828-212-4185

7. **Medication
   Assistance Program**
   Burke County Department of
   Social Services
   700 E. Parker Rd.
   Morganton, NC 28655
   828-764-9600

   Burke County Medicaid/
   Medicare Services
   828-439-2000

   Burke County
   Prescription Assistance
   877-321-2652

8. **Employment/ Vocational
   Rehab/ Education**
   NC Works Career Center/ ESC
   720 E. Union St.
   Morganton, NC 28655
   828-438-6161

Western Regional Vocational
Rehabilitation Services
200 Enola Road
Morganton, NC 28655
828-433-2423 or 828-608-5600

9. **Legal Services**
   Legal Aid of NC
   211 E. Union St.
   Morganton, NC 28655
   828-437-8280 or 800-849-5195

10. **Recreational/ Leisure**
    Morganton/Burke County
    Visitor Information Center
    110 E. Meeting St.
    Morganton, NC 28655
    828-433-6793

11. **Special Populations**
    Morganton/Burke
    Senior Center
    501 N. Green St.
    Morganton, NC 28655
    828-430-4147

    Option (Domestic Violence)
    828-438-9444

    Poison Control Center
    800-222-1222

    Veterans Administration
    110 S. Green St.
    Morganton, North Carolina
    828-439-4373

CHAPTER 13

Cabarrus County

1. Mental Health and Crisis Services
Atrium Behavioral Health
301 Medical Park Dr., #202
Concord, North Carolina
704-403-2626 or 800-418-2065

Piedmont Behavioral Health
245 Le Phillip Court, NE
Concord, North Carolina
704-721-7000

National Alliance on
Mental Illness
704-963-9199 or 800-451-9682

2. Substance Abuse Services
DayMark Recovery Services
284 Executive Branch Dr.,
Suite 100
Concord, NC 28025
704-939-1100

3. Clothing/ Food Assistance/ Financial Services
Clothing Closet
72 Corbin Ave., NW
Concord, NC 28025
704-786-4020

Meals on Wheels
1701 S. Main St.
Kannapolis, NC 28083
704-932-3412

Salvation Army (clothing)
216 Patterson Ave.
Concord, NC 28025
704-782-7822

Samaritan House Soup Kitchen
216 Patterson Ave.
Concord, NC 28025
704-782-7822

4. Housing and Shelters
Concord Housing Authority
283 Harold Goodman
Circle, SW
Concord, North Carolina
704-920-6100

Samaritan House (Shelter)
216 Patterson Ave.
Concord, NC 28025
704-490-4250

Cabarrus Victim's Assistance
704-782-0227

5. **Transportation**
Cabarrus County
Transportation Services
(CCTS)
135 Cabarrus Ave., E #101
Concord, NC 28025
704-920-2246

6. **Medical Services**
Community Free Clinic
528-A Lake Concord Road
Concord, NC 28025
704-782-0650

7. **Medication
Assistance Program**
Cabarrus County Department
of Social Services
1303 S. Cannon Blvd.
Kannapolis, NC 28083
704-920-1400

8. **Employment/ Vocational
Rehab/ Education**
NC Works Career Center
845 Church St., N
Suite 201
Concord, NC 28025
704-786-3183

Vocational Rehabilitation
820 Florence St., NW
Concord, NC 28025
704-706-6850

9. **Legal Services**
Legal Aid
785 Davidson Dr., NW
Concord, NC 28025
704-786-4145 or 800-849-8009

Legal Aid of NC
363 Church St., N.
Suite 200
Concord, NC 28025
866-219-5262

10. **Recreational/ Leisure**
Cabarrus County Convention
and Visitors Bureau
10099 Weddington Rd.,
Suite 102
Concord, NC 28027
704-782-4340

11. **Special Populations**
Cabarrus County
Veterans Services-
The Old Creamery
363 Church St., N., #180
Concord, NC 28025
704-920-2869

Cabarrus Victims Assistance
Network (CVAN)
704-788-2826

Department of Aging
1303 S. Cannon Blvd.
Kannapolis, NC 28083
704-920-1400

Senior Center of
Cabarrus County
331 Corbin Ave., SE
Concord, NC 28025
704-920-3484

CHAPTER 14

Caldwell County

1. **Mental Health and Crisis Services**
Foothills Area Authority, LME-
Burke County
306 S. King St.
Morganton, North Carolina
828-432-2846

2. **Substance Abuse Services**
Bethel Colony of Mercy
1675 Bethel Colony Road
Lenoir, NC 28645
828-754-3781

Caldwell Halfway House (Men)
951 Kenham Pl.
Lenoir , NC 28645
828-754-5148

Mental Health/Substance Abuse
Program of Caldwell County
828-754-4551

VAYA Health
825 Wilkesboro Blvd., NE
Lenoir, NC 28645
800-849-6127

3. **Clothing/ Food Assistance/ Financial Services**
Angel Food Ministries
828-758-5476

Caldwell County
Yolkfellow, Inc.
202 Harper Ave.
Lenoir, NC 28645
828-754-7088

Crossroads Church
(Food Pantry)
2075 Morganton Blvd.
Lenoir, NC 28645
828-612-6802

Dualtown Outreach
Center, Inc.
1302 Norwood St., SW
Lenoir, NC 28645
828-758-2482

Goodwill (Clothing)
3076 Hickory Blvd.
Hudson, NC 28638
828-726-5944

Lenoir Soup Kitchen
1113 College Ave., SW
Lenoir, NC 28645
828-758-1411

Mountain Grove Baptist
Church (Food Pantry)
2485 Connelly Springs Rd.
Granite Falls, NC 28630
828-728-9557

South Caldwell Christian
Ministries (Clothing)
5 Quarry Rd.
Granite Falls, NC 28630
828-396-4000

United Way of Caldwell County
304 Main St., SW, Suite 404
& 406
Lenoir, NC 28645
828-758-9300

WIC Clinic
828-426-8407

4. *Housing and Shelters*
American Red Cross (Disasters/
Emergencies)
1144 Morganton Blvd., SW
Lenoir, NC 28645
800-733-2767

Lenoir Housing Authority
431 Vance St., NW
Lenoir, NC 28645
828-758-5536

Lenoir Emergency
Outreach Shelter
1129 West Ave.
Lenoir, NC 28645
828-76-3634

NC Housing Coalition
888-313-4956

NC Housing Search
877-428-8844

Salvation Army
(Housing Assistance)
4370 Hickory Blvd.
Granite Falls, NC 28630
828-496-2370

Shelter Home of
Caldwell County
907 Harper Ave., SW
Lenoir, NC 28645
828-758-0888

5. *Transportation*
Caldwell County Area Transit
System Inc.
214 Mulberry St., NW
Lenoir, NC 28645
828-757-4888

Green Way Transit (Seniors)
828-464-9444

Greenway
Public Transportation
1214 Blowing Rock Blvd.
Lenoir, NC 28645
828-757-8679

6. *Medical Services*
Caldwell County
Health Department
2345 Morganton Blvd., SW
Suite B
Lenoir, NC 28645
828-426-8400

Helping Hands Clinic
810 Harper Ave., NW
Lenoir, NC 28645
828-754-8565

7. *Medication*
Assistance Program
Caldwell County Department
of Social Services
2345 Morganton Blvd., SW
Suite A
Lenoir, NC 28645
828-426-8200

NeedyMeds
800-503-6897

8. *Employment/ Vocational*
Rehab/ Education
Caldwell County Joblink
Center- (ESC)
504 Wilkesboro Blvd., SE
Lenoir, NC 28645
828-757-5622

Division of
Vocational Rehabilitation
675 Pennton Ave., SW
Lenoir, NC 28645
828-572-6600

Goodwill Industries
960 Blowing Rock Blvd., NE
Lenoir, NC 28645
828-758-7715

NC Works Career Center
1913 Hickory Boulevard
Lenoir, NC 28645
828-759-4680

9. *Legal Services*
Catawba Valley Legal Services,
Inc.-Burke County
Morganton, North Carolina
828-437-8280

Legal Aid-Burke County
211 E. Union St.
Morganton, North Carolina
828-437-8280 or 800-849-5195

NC Lawyer Referral Services
800-662-7660

Senior Citizens Legal Services
828-722-7140

10. *Recreational/ Leisure*
Caldwell County
Visitors Center
1909 Hickory Blvd.
Lenoir, NC 28645
828-726-0616

11. *Special Populations*
Caldwell Senior Center
650 A Pennton Ave., SW
Lenoir, NC 28645
828-758-2883

Caldwell County
Veterans Office
905 West Ave., NW
Lenoir, NC 28645
828-757-1345

CHAPTER 15

Camden County

1. **Mental Health and Crisis Services**
Albemarle Mental Health Center-Pasquotank County
1141 N. Road Street
Elizabeth City, NC 27909
252-338-8352

East Carolina Behavioral Health-Hertford County
144 Community College Rd.
Ahoskie, NC 27910
252-332-4137

2. **Substance Abuse Services**
Mental Health/Substance Abuse Program
Camden County,
North Carolina
252-335-5158

3. **Clothing/ Food Assistance/ Financial Services**
Camden Food Pantry
Camden Methodist Church
197 N. Carolina Hwy.
343, South
Camden, NC 27921
252-335-7565

Food Bank of the Albemarle
252-335-4035

Mount Zion Church of God-Food Distribution Center
118 NC Highway 343, South
Camden, NC 27921
252-331-2176

Salvation Army
252-338-6780

United Way
252-333-1510

WIC Clinic
252-338-4460

4. **Housing and Shelters**
Albemarle Hopeline-
Pasquotank County (Domestic
Violence Shelter)
Elizabeth City, North Carolina
252-338-3011

Catholic Charities
252-426-7717

5. **Transportation**
Gates Inter-Transportation
System (GITS)- Gates County
714 Main St.
Gatesville, NC 27938
252-357-4487

Inter-County Public
Transportation Authority
(ICPTA)-Pasquotank County
110 Kitty Hawk Ln.
Elizabeth City, NC 27909
252-338-4480

6. **Medical Services**
Camden County
Health Department
160 US Highway 158, East
Camden, NC 27921
252-338-4460

Albemarle Regional Health
Services-Pasquotank County
711 Roanoke Ave.
Elizabeth City, NC 27909
252-338-4400 or 252-338-4460

7. **Medication Assistance Program**
Camden County Department of
Social Services
117 N. NC Highway 343
Camden, NC 27921
252-338-1919 or 252-331-4787

GoodRx
855-268-2822

NeedyMeds
800-503-6897

8. **Employment/ Vocational Rehab/ Education**
JobLink Center/ NC Works
Career Center
422 McArthur Street
Elizabeth City, NC 27909
252-331-4798

Vocational Rehabilitation-
Pasquotank County
401 S. Griffin St., Suite 100
Elizabeth City, NC 27909
252-331-4768

9. **Legal Services**
Legal Services of the Coastal
Plains-Hertford County
610 Church St., East
Ahoskie, NC 27910
252-332-5124, 800-682-0010,
or 866-219-5262

10. *Recreational/Leisure*

Dismal Swamp Canal
Welcome Center
2356 US Highway 17
South Mills, NC 27976
252-771-8333

Dismal Swamp State Park
2294 US 17, North
South Mills NC 27976
252-771-6593

11. *Special Populations*

Camden County Center for
Active Adults
252-335-2569

Camden County Senior Center
117 NC Highway 343, North
Camden, NC 27921
252-333-3226 or 252-338-1919,
ext. 248

Veterans Services-
Pasquotank County
1023 Highway 17, South
Elizabeth City, NC 27909
252-331-4741

CHAPTER 16

Carteret County

1. **Mental Health and Crisis Services**
Coast Care-New Hanover County
3809 Shipyard Boulevard
Wilmington, North Carolina
910-550-2600

East Carolina Behavioral
Health-Craven County
P.O. Box 1636
New Bern, NC 29563
252-636-1510 or 877-685-2415

PORT Health
3715 Guardian Ave.
Morehead City, NC 28557
252-222-3144

RHA Health Services
Mobile Cruise Line
844-709-4097

Trillium Mobile
Morehead City, North Carolina
Crisis Line 877-685-2415

2. **Substance Abuse Services**
AA-Morehead City
252-726-8540

Le'Chris/Crisis Intervention
229 Professional Cir., Suite 3
Morehead City, NC 28557
252-726-9006

Peer Recovery Center
252-222-3888

Step Out Counseling Center
207 N. 35th St.
Morehead City, NC 28557
252-726-3554

3. **Clothing/ Food Assistance/ Financial Services**
Loaves and Fishes
Beaufort, North Carolina
252-504-0123

Martha's Mission Cupboard
901 Bay St.
Morehead City, NC 28557
252-726-1717

Meals on Wheels- Cape
Carteret/Emerald Isle
252-241-5282

Salvation Army
1700 Arendell St.
Morehead City, NC 28557
752-726-7147

Soup Kitchen/Hope Mission
1410 Bridges St.
Morehead City, North Carolina
252-240-2359 or 252-247-2543

Second Blessings (Clothing)
5178 Highway 70 W., Suite B
Morehead City, NC 28557
252-726-7921

Storehouse Food Pantry
3114 Bridges St.
Morehead City, North Carolina
252-725-5539

WIC Clinic
252-728-8550

4. *Housing and Shelters*
Beaufort Housing Authority
716 Mulberry St.
Beaufort, NC 28516
252-728-3226

Catholic Charities
252-638-2188

Caroline's House
(Emergency Shelter)
252-726-2336

Coastal Community Action
252-223-1630

Coastal Women's Shelter-
Craven County
New Bern, North Carolina
252-638-4509

East Carolina Regional
Housing Authority
2204 Bay St.
Morehead City, North Carolina
252-726-4401

Hope Mission (Emergency
Men Shelter)
1410 Bridges St.
Morehead City, NC 28557
252-240-2359 or 252-515-6361

Step Forward
Transitional Housing
252-726-1076

5. *Transportation*
Carteret County Area
Transportation System
(CCATS)
2820 Bridges St., Suite A
Morehead City, NC 28557
252-240-1043

Coastal Community Action
(Seniors)
Newport, North Carolina
252-223-1630

Crystal Coast
Medical Transport
252-808-5555

Friendly
Medical Transportation
252-808-3400

Retired Senior Volunteer Program (RSVP)
252-223-1652

6. **Medical Services**
Carteret County
Health Department
3820 Bridges St., Suite A
Morehead City, NC 28557
252-728-8550

Broad Street Clinic
534 N. 35th St.
Morehead City, NC 28557
252-726-4562

Harker's Island UMC
252-728-7015

Snug Harbor on Nelson Bay
(Physical Therapy)
Sea Level, NC
252-225-4411

7. **Medication Assistance Program**
DSS-Beaufort County
210 Craven St.
Beaufort, NC 28516
252-728-3181

GoodRx
855-268-2822

8. **Employment/ Vocational Rehab/ Education**
Employment Security
Commission/ JobLink Center
309 Commerce Ave.
Morehead City, NC 28557
252-726-7151

NC Works Career Center
252-222-6038

Vocational Rehabilitation
310 Commerce Ave., Suite A
Morehead City, NC 28557
252-247-2037

9. **Legal Services**
Legal Aid of NC-Pitt County
301 Evans St., Suite 102
Greenville, NC 27858
252-758-0113 or 800-682-4592

Pamlico Sound Legal Services-
Craven County
213 Pollock St.
New Bern, NC 28560
919-637-9502, 866-219-5262,
or 800-672-8213

10. **Recreational/ Leisure**
Atlantic Beach Town Park
915 W. Fort Macon Rd.
Atlantic Beach, North
Carolina's
252-726-4456

Emerald Isle Parks
and Recreation
Emerald Isle, North Carolina
252-354-6350

Fort Benjamin Park
Recreation Center
Newport, North Carolina
252-222-5858

North Carolina Aquarium
1 Roosevelt Blvd.
Pine Knoll Shores, NC 28512
252-247-4003

Visitors Center's
3409 Arendell St.
Morehead City, North Carolina
252-726-8148

Western Park
Community Center
Cedar Point, North Carolina
252-393-1481

11. *Special Populations*
Carteret County Domestic
Violence Program
252-726-2336 or (Crisis Line)
252-728-3788

Leon Mann Enrichment Center
(Seniors)
3820 Galantis Drive
Morehead City, NC 28557
252-247-2626

Special Olympics of
Carteret County
Beaufort, North Carolina
252-222-5858

Veterans Affairs
5420 US Highway 70, West
Morehead City, NC 28577
252-240-2349

Veterans Services
3710-B John Platt Drive
Morehead City, North Carolina
252-728-8440

CHAPTER 17

Caswell County

1. ***Mental Health and Crisis Services***
Alamance-Caswell, Local Management Entity (LME)
319 Graham-Hopedale Road
Burlington, North Carolina
336-513-4200

2. ***Substance Abuse Services***
Caswell Clinic
339 Wall Street
Yanceyville, NC 27379
336-694-4141

   Sandhill Center-
Guilford County
201 N. Eugene St.
Greensboro, NC 27401

3. ***Clothing/ Food Assistance/ Financial Services***
Caswell County Outreach Ministries (Clothes)
225 3rd Ave.
Yanceyville, NC 27379
336-694-1255

   Caswell Parish and Two Hearts Drift Store (Food/Clothes)
1038 Main St.
Yanceyville, NC 27379
336-694-6428

   WIC Program
336-694-7141

4. ***Housing and Shelters***
Caswell County Outreach Housing (Section 8 Housing)
205 E. Church St.
Yanceyville, NC 27379
336-694-9318

   Caswell Family Violence
P.O. Box 639
Yanceyville, North Carolina
336-694-5655

   Homeless Liaison- Caswell County SD (Youth)
319 Main St.
Yanceyville, NC 27379
336-694-4112

5. **Transportation**
Caswell County Area
Transportation System (CATS)
206 County Park Rd.
Yanceyville, NC 27379
336-694-1424

Pelham Transportation-
Rockingham County
336-349-7113

6. **Medical Services**
Caswell County
Health Department
189 County Park Rd.
Yanceyville, NC 27379
336-694-4129

7. **Medication
Assistance Program**
Caswell County Department of
Social Services
175 E. Church St.
Yanceyville, NC 27379
336-694-4141

8. **Employment/ Vocational
Rehab/ Education**
NC Works Career Center
331 Piedmont Dr.
Yanceyville, NC 27379
336-646-2806

NC Vocational Rehabilitation-
Rockingham County
800-638-5643

9. **Legal Services**
Legal Aid of NC-
Durham County
201 W. Main St., Suite 400
Durham, North Carolina
919-688-6396

Legal Aid of NC-
Guilford County
122 N. Elm St., Suite 700
Greensboro, NC 27401
336-272-0148 or 800-951-2257

10. **Recreational/ Leisure**
Caswell County Parks and
Recreation Center
228 County Park Rd.
Yanceyville, NC 27379
336-694-4449

Caswell Visitor Center
(Bidirectional Rest Area)/
(Located 2 miles south of Va
Stateline, on exit 29.)
NC US 29
Caswell County-
North Carolina
Piedmont Triad Visitor Center
700 NC Highway 700
Pelham, NC 27311
336-388-9830

11. **Special Populations**
Caswell County Senior Center
649 Fire Tower Rd.
Yanceyville, NC 27379
336-694-7447

Veterans Service Office
175 E. Church St.
Yanceyville, NC 27379
336-694-4141

CHAPTER 18

Catawba County

1. **Mental Health and Crisis Services**
Catawba Valley
Behavioral Health
327 1st Ave., NW
Hickory, North Carolina
828-695-5900 or (Mobile Crisis) 888-235-4673

Cognitive Connections
1109 2nd Ave., SW
Hickory, NC 28602
828-327-6026

Cornerstone Counseling Center
828-322-4941

Family Guidance Center
17 US Highway 70, SE
Hickory, NC 28602
828-322-1400

2. **Substance Abuse Services**
Catawba Science Center
243 3rd Ave., NE
Hickory, NC 28601
828-322-8169

Catawba Valley Health Services
-Health First Center
828-485-2300

Mental Health/Substance
Abuse Program
Catawba County,
North Carolina
828-326-5900

Partners Behavioral
Health Management
1985 Tate Blvd., SE
Hickory, NC 28602
828-327-2595 or 888-235-4673
(Crisis Line)

3. **Clothing/ Food Assistance/ Financial Services**
Christian Food Pantry
2211 Hopewell Church Road
Sherrills Ford, North Carolina
704-877-0404

Hickory PORCH
(Food Assistance)
2505 1st Ave., SW
Hickory, North Carolina
828-327-4286

Hickory Soup Kitchen
131 Main Ave., NE
Hickory, NC 28601
828-327-4828

Highways and Hedges Ministry
3675 Herman Sipe Rd.
Conover, NC 28613
828-781-8095

Meals on Wheels (Seniors)
828-695-5610

New Hope Homeless and
Poverty Ministry- (Mobile
Food Pantry)
828-781-3789

Safe Harbor Rescue Mission
112 2nd Ave., SE
Hickory, NC 28602
828-326-7233

Sherrills Ford Community
Food Pantry
Sherrills Ford, North Carolina
828-478-9625

St. John's Lutheran Church
2126 Saint Johns Church
Rd., NE
Conover, North Carolina
828-464-4071

The Corner Table Soup Kitchen
112 N. Main Ave.
Newton, North Carolina
828-464-0355

WIC Clinic
828-695-5884

4. *Housing and Shelters*

Catholic Charities
800-227-7261

Exodus Homes (Recovery)
122 8th Avenue Drive, SW
Hickory, NC 28602
828-324-4870

Family Guidance Center
(Women Shelter)
17 US Highway 70, SE
Hickory, NC 28602
828-327-1400

Hickory Housing Authority
841 S. Center St.
Hickory, NC 28602
828-328-5373

Life House (Shelter)
828-575-6088

Oxford House-Grace
822 7th Avenue Place, SW
Hickory, NC 28602
828-855-1427

Oxford House-Viewmont
326 25th Ave., NW
Hickory, NC 28601
828-855-1016

Shelter of Hope/Salvation Army
760 3rd Avenue Place, SE
Hickory, NC 28602
828-322-8061

5. *Transportation*
Greenway
Public Transportation
1515 4th St., SW
Conover, North Carolina
828-465-7634 or 828-464-9444

6. *Medical Services*
Catawba County
Health Department
3070 11th Avenue Drive, SE
Hickory, NC 28602
828-695-5800

Catawba Valley Medical
Center-ER
828-326-3850

Frye Regional Medical
Center- ER
828-315-3190

7. *Medication
Assistance Program*
AIDS Leadership Foothills Area
Alliance (ALFAA)
1120 Fairgrove Church
Road, SE
Suite 28
Hickory, NC 28602
828-322-1447

Catawba County Department
of Social Services
3030 11th Avenue Drive, SE
Hickory, NC 28602
828-695-5600

8. *Employment/ Vocational
Rehab/ Education*
NC Works Career Center
3301 Highway 70, SE
Newton, NC 28658
828-466-5535

Vocational Rehabilitation
1261 10th Avenue Lane, SE
Hickory, NC 28602
828-322-2921

9. *Legal Services*
Legal Aid of NC
800-849-5195
Legal Aid of North Carolina-
Burke County
211 E. Union St.
Morganton, NC 28655
828-437-8280 or 866-219-5262

10. *Recreational/ Leisure*
Visitors Information Center
1055 Southgate Corporate
Park, SW
Hickory, NC 28602
828-328-6111

11. *Special Populations*
Catawba County
Veterans Services
100 Southwest Boulevard
Newton, NC 28658
828-465-8255

West Hickory Senior Center
400 17th St., SW
Hickory, NC 28602
828-328-2269

Westmont Senior Center
1316 Main Avenue Drive, NW
Hickory, NC 28601
828-324-1200

CHAPTER 19

Chatham County

1. Mental Health and Crisis Services
Carolina Counseling Services
68 Fayetteville St.
Pittsboro, North Carolina
919-944-7200

El Futuro (Latino Services)
401-B N. Ivy Ave.
Siler City, North Carolina
919-742-5262 or 919-799-2625

OPC MH/DD/SA Authority-
Orange County
100 Europa Dr., Suite 490
Chapel Hill, North Carolina
919-913-4000

2. Substance Abuse Services
Alcoholics Anonymous
888-237-3235
Chatham Counseling Center of
Freedom House
919-542-4422

Chatham Recovery
1758 E. 11th St., Suite E
Siler City, North Carolina
919-663-3303

DayMark Recovery Services
1105 E. Cardinal St.
Siler City, North Carolina
919-663-2955

Project Turnaround
(Adolescents)
919-932-2930

3. Clothing/ Food Assistance/ Financial Services
CORA Food Pantry
40 Camp Drive
Pittsboro, North Carolina
919-542-5020

Salvation Army
Siler City, North Carolina
919-663-0443

West Chatham Food Pantry
2535 Old US Highway
421, North
Siler City, NC 27344
919-742-3111

WIC Program
7278 Pittsboro Moncure Rd.
Moncure, North Carolina
919-742-5602

WIC Program
224 S. 10th Ave.
Siler City, North Carolina
919-663-1744

United Way
919-542-1110

4. *Housing and Shelters*
    Catholic Charities
    919-286-1964

    Central Piedmont
    Community Action
    919-542-4781

    Chatham County
    Housing Authority
    13450 US Highway 64
    Siler City, NC 27344
    919-742-1236 or 919-542-3742

    Salvation Army
    919-548-6856 or 919-542-1593

5. *Transportation*
    Chatham Transit Network
    480 Hillsboro St., Building F
    Pittsboro, North Carolina
    919-542-5136

6. *Medical Services*
    Chatham County
    Health Department
    80 East St.
    Pittsboro, North Carolina
    919-542-8215 or 919-542-8220

    Siler City Community
    Health Center
    4013 N. Ivy Avenue
    Siler City, North Carolina
    919-663-1744

7. *Medication*
    Assistance Program
    Chatham County Department
    of Social Services
    102 Camp Drive
    Pittsboro, NC 27312
    919-542-2759 or 919-542-2911
    (Emergency Line)

8. *Employment/ Vocational*
    Rehab/ Education
    Employment
    Security Commission
    205 Chatham Sq.
    Siler City, NC 27344
    919-742-7454

    JobLink Center
    35 W. Chatham St.
    Pittsboro, NC 27312
    919-542-4781

    Vocational Rehabilitation
    505 MLK Boulevard
    Siler City, North Carolina
    919-663-2544

9. ***Legal Services***
Legal Aid of NC
959 East St., Suite A & B
Pittsboro, North Carolina
919-542-0475

10. ***Recreational/ Leisure***
Chatham County Convention
and Visitors Bureau
964 East St., Suite 204
Pittsboro, NC 27312
919-542-8296 or 800-316-3829

11. ***Special Populations***
Crisis Helpline
919-929-0479

Family Violence and Rape
Crisis Services
919-545-0224 (Crisis Line)

Eastern Chatham Senior
Center/Chatham Council
of Aging
365 NC Highway 87, North
Pittsboro, NC 27312
919-542-4512

Second Bloom of Chatham
(Domestic Violence)
14 N. Small St.
Pittsboro, NC 27312
Helpline 919-545-0005

Veteran Services
Office-Chatham
15 South St.
Pittsboro, North Carolina
919-542-8202

Western Chatham
Senior Center
112 Village Lake Rd.
Siler City, NC 27344
919-742-3975

CHAPTER 20

Cherokee County

1. **Mental Health and Crisis Services**
Appalachian
Community Services
750 US Highway 64 W.
Murphy, NC 28906
828-837-0071

   Community Corrections
21 Peachtree St.
Murphy, NC 28906
828-837-5827

2. **Substance Abuse Services**
VAYA Health
750 US Highway 64 W.
Murphy, NC 28906
800-849-6127

   Appalachian
Community Services
Crisis Line-888-315-2880

   Mental Health/Substance Abuse
Program Cherokee County
828-837-7466

3. **Clothing/ Food Assistance/ Financial Services**
Cherokee County Food
Bank-Andrews
828-321-5512

   MANNA Food Distribution
1212 Bird Town Road
Cherokee, NC 28719
828-299-3663

4. **Housing and Shelters**
Housing Authority-Andrews
291 Whitaker Ln.
Andrews, NC 28901
828-321-5257

   Housing Authority-Murphy
80 Beal Cir.
Murphy, NC 28906
828-837-6662

5. **Transportation**
Cherokee County Transit
77 Hardin St.
Murphy, NC 28906
828-837-1789

6. **Medical Services**
   Health Department
   (Murphy Office)
   228 Hilton St.
   Murphy, NC 28906
   828-837-7486

7. **Medication
   Assistance Program**
   Cherokee County Department
   of Social Services
   40 Peachtree St.
   Murphy, NC 28906
   828-837-7455

8. **Employment/ Vocational
   Rehab/ Education**
   Cherokee County
   Joblink Center
   642 Murphy Rd.
   Murphy, NC 28906
   828-837-7407

   NC Vocational Rehabilitation
   510 E. US Highway 64 Alt.
   Murphy, NC 28906
   828-837-6218

9. **Legal Services**
   Western NC Legal Services-
   Jackson County
   Sylva, North Carolina
   704-586-8931

10. **Recreational/ Leisure**
    Cherokee County
    Visitor Center
    20 Tennessee St.
    Murphy, NC 28906
    828-557-0602 or 800-VISIT NC

11. **Special Populations**
    Cherokee County Veterans
    Administration Office
    75 Peachtree St.
    Murphy, NC 28906
    828-835-8663

    Cherokee County Senior Center
    69 Alpine St.
    Murphy, NC 28906
    828-837-2467

    REACH, Inc.
    (Domestic Violence)
    84 Valley River Ave.
    Murphy, NC 28906
    828-835-3434

    Veteran Services
    98 Hickory St.
    Murphy, NC 28906
    828-837-2616

CHAPTER 21

Chowan County

1. **Mental Health and Crisis Services**
Chowan Vidant
Emergency Room
211 Virginia Rd.
Edenton, NC 27932
252-482-6219

East Carolina Behavioral
Health, LME-Craven County
800 Cardinal Rd.
New Bern, NC 28563
252-636-1510

2. **Substance Abuse Services**
AA
252-338-1849 or 800-350-2538

Port Health Services-
Pasquotank County
1141 N. Road Street, Suite L
Elizabeth City, NC 27909
252-335-0803

3. **Clothing/ Food Assistance/ Financial Services**
Edenton-Chowan County
Food Pantry
1370 N. Broad Street
Edenton, NC 27932
252-482-2504

Food Bank of Albemarle-
Pasquotank County
100 Tidewater Way
Elizabeth City, NC 27909
252-335-4035

4. **Housing and Shelters**
Edenton Housing Authority
115 Blades St.
Edenton, NC 27932
252-482-8165

5. **Transportation**
Gates Enter-Regional
Transportation System-
Gates County
714 Main St.
Gatesville, NC 27938
252-357-4487

6. **Medical Services**
Chowan County
Health Department
202 W. Hicks St.
Edenton, NC 27932
252-482-6003

Chowan Hospital
211 Virginia Rd.
Edenton, NC 27932
252-482-8451

Community Care Clinic
2869 Virginia Rd.
Tyner, NC 27980
252-384-4733

7. **Medication
Assistance Program**
Chowan County Department of
Social Services
100 W. Freemason Circle
Edenton, NC 27932
252-482-7441

GoodRx
855-26 8-2822

Needy Meds
800-503-6897

8. **Employment/ Vocational
Rehab/ Education**
Economic
Improvement Council
712 Virginia Rd.
Edenton, NC 27932
252-482-4495

NC Works Center
118 Blades St., Building 3,
Room 300
Edenton, NC 27932
252-482-2195

Vocational Rehabilitation
401 S. Griffin St., Suite 100
Elizabeth City, NC 27909
252-331-4768

9. **Legal Services**
Legal Aid of
NC-Hertford County
610 E. Church St.
Ahoskie, NC 27910
252-332-5124

10. **Recreational/ Leisure**
Edenton Parks and
Recreation Department
703 N. Granville St.
Edenton, NC 27932
252-482-8595

Northern Chowan
Community Center
2869 Virginia Rd.
Tyner, NC 27980
252-221-4901

Walker Community Center
824 N. Oakum St.
Edenton, NC 27932
Visitor Center
101 W. Water St.
Edenton, NC 27932
252-482-0300

11. *Special Populations*

Senior Center
204 E. Church St.
Edenton, NC 27932
252-482-2242

Veterans Services
305 W. Freemason St.
Edenton, NC 27932
252-482-1033

CHAPTER 22

Clay County

1. **Mental Health and Crisis Services**
First at Blue Ridge
32 Knox Rd.
Ridgecrest, NC 28770
828-669-0011

2. **Substance Abuse Services**
Smokey Mountain Center,
LME-Jackson County
44 Bonnie Ln.
Sylva, NC 28779
828-586-5501

3. **Clothing/ Food Assistance/ Financial Services**
Clay County Food Pantry
(CCFP)
2278 Hinton Center Rd.
Hayesville, NC 28904
828-389-1657

WIC Clinic
828-389-8052, extension 20

*For info on Soup Kitchens
call 211 or 888-892-1162

4. **Housing and Shelters**
Clay County Housing Authority
800-685-8470

Four Square Community
Action-Cherokee County
61 Milton Mashburn Drive
Andrews, NC 28901
828-389-6757

5. **Transportation**
Clay County Transportation
P.O. Box 118
Hayesville, NC 28904
828-389-0644

6. **Medical Services**
Clay County
Health Department
1 Riverside Circle
Hayesville, NC 28904
828-389-8052

7. *Medication Assistance Program*
Clay County Department of
Social Services
55 Riverside Cir.
Hayesville, NC 28904
828-389-6301

8. *Employment/ Vocational Rehab/ Education*
NC JobLink-Clay County
56 Riverside Cir.
Hayesville, NC 28904
828-389-6301

9. *Legal Services*
Sylva Legal Aid-Jackson County
1286 W. Main St.
Sylva, North Carolina
828-586-8931

Legal Aid of NC
828-389-2399

10. *Recreational/ Leisure*
Clay County Chamber
of Commerce
96 Sanderson St.
Hayesville, NC 28904
828-389-3704

Smoky Mountain Visitors
Center-Macon County
4437 Georgia Rd.
Franklin, NC 28734
828-369-9606

Warne Community Center
4759 Old Hwy. 64, West
Warne, NC 28909
828-389-2586

11. *Special Populations*
Clay County Senior Center
196 Ritter Rd.
Hayesville, North Carolina
828-389-9271

REACH of Clay County
(Domestic Violence)
P.O. Box 1485
Hayesville, North Carolina
Crisis Line-828-389-0797

Veterans Services
54 Church St.
Hayesville, NC 28904
828-389-3355

CHAPTER 23

Cleveland County

1. *Mental Health and Crisis Services*

Adventure House
924 N. Lafayette St.
Shelby, NC 28150
704-482-3370

Mental Health Association
215 E. Warren St.
Shelby, North Carolina
704-481-8637

Ollie Harris Behavioral
Health Center
200 S. Post Rd., #2
Shelby, NC 20152
704-600-6900

Pathways Mental Health, LME
124 S. Post Rd.
Shelby, NC 28152
704-476-4131

Pathways MH/DD/SA Center
917 1st St.
Shelby, NC 28150
704-476-4052

2. *Substance Abuse Services*

Crossroads Rescue Mission
206 Mount Sinai Church Road
Shelby, NC 28152
704-484-8770

Kings Mountain Crisis Ministry
208 N. Cleveland Ave.
Kings Mountain, NC 28086
704-739-7256

Mental Health/Substance
Abuse Program
Cleveland County,
North Carolina
704-484-6400

Substance Abuse
Prevention Coalition
315 E. Grover St.
Shelby, NC 28150
704-484-5199

3. ***Clothing/ Food Assistance/ Financial Services***
American Red Cross
(Emergency Assistance)
1333 Falls Town Rd.-Highway 18, North
Shelby, NC 28150
704-487-8594

Boiling Springs Baptist
(Food Pantry)
307 S. Main St.
Boiling Springs, North Carolina
704-434-6244

Greater Cleveland County
Baptist Association
1175 Wyke Rd.
Shelby, NC 28150
704-481-9119

Friendship United Methodist
Church (Food Pantry)
111 Friendship Drive
Fallston, NC 28042
704-538-9270

Rise N Shine Farms, LLC
215 Turner Rd.
Casar, NC 28020
704-692-0005

Salvation Army
311 N. Lafayette St.
Shelby, NC 28150
704-482-0375

UCAN, Inc.
The Bliss Center
230 E. Main St.
Lawndale, NC 28090
704-538-8417

WIC Program
980-484-5170

4. ***Housing and Shelters***
Cleveland County Abuse
Prevention Council- (Domestic Violence Shelter)
407 W. Warren St.
Shelby, NC 28150
704-487-9325 or 704-481-0043
(Hotline)

Cleveland County Rescue
Mission (Women/
Children Shelter)
1100 Buffalo St.
Shelby, NC 28150
704-481-1889

Grace of God Rescue Mission
537 W. Main St.
Forrest City, NC 28043
828-245-9141

Kings Mountain Housing
201 McGill Ct.
Kings Mountain, NC 28086
704-739-2816

Section 8 Housing Program
704-487-0476

Victim and Community
Shelby, NC 28151
704-484-8604

5. **Transportation**
Cleveland County Transit
(CCT)/ REACH
952 Airport Rd.
Shelby, NC 28150
704-482-6465

6. **Medical Services**
Cleveland County
Health Department
200 S. Post Rd.,
Shelby, NC 28152
704-484-5100

Kings Mountain Hospital
706 W. King St.
Kings Mountain, NC 28086
980-487-5000

7. **Medication
Assistance Program**
Cleveland County Department
of Social Services
130 S. Post Rd.
Shelby, NC 28151
704-487-0661

GoodRx
855-268-2822

8. **Employment/ Vocational
Rehab/ Education**
JobLink Center
201 W. Marion St., Suite 319
Shelby, NC 28150
704-480-1268

NC Works Career Center
404 E. Marion St.
Shelby, NC 28150
704-480-5414

NC Vocational
Rehabilitation Office
1427 E. Marion St.
Shelby, NC 28150
704-480-5412

9. **Legal Services**
Catawba Valley Legal Services,
Inc.-Burke County
Morganton, North Carolina
828-437-8280

Legal Aid- Gaston County
1508 S. York Rd.
Gastonia, NC 28052
704-865-2357 or 800-230-5812

10. **Recreational/ Leisure**
Cleveland County Chamber
Travel and Tourism
2001 E. Dixon Blvd.
Shelby, NC 28152
704-482-7882

NC Welcome Center
2345 US Highway Interstate 85
Kings Mountain, NC 28086
704-937-7861

Visitors Center
200 S. Lafayette St.
Shelby, NC 28150
704-484-4804

YMCA
411 Cherryville Rd.
Shelby, NC 28150
704-484-9622

11. Special Populations

Cleveland County Heart and
Hooves (Disabled Children)
North Shelby School
1205 North Side Dr.
Shelby, NC 28150
704-487-9941

Leona Neal Senior Center
100 T.R. Harris Drive
Shelby, NC 28150
704-482-3488

H.L. Patrick Senior Center
909 E. Kings St.
Kings Mountain, NC 28086
704-734-0447

NC Services for the Blind
130 S. Post Rd.
Shelby, NC 28150
704-487-0661

Veterans Services Office
311 E. Marion St.
Shelby, NC 28150
704-484-4803

CHAPTER 24

Columbus County

1. **Mental Health and Crisis Services**
Advantage
Behavioral Healthcare
732 Davis Ave.
Whiteville, North Carolina
910-640-1038

Coastal Southeastern
United Care
100 Memory Plaza, #A
Whiteville, North Carolina
910-640-2230

H & H Mental Health
174 Biltmore Rd.
Whiteville, North Carolina
910-640-1830

Life Changing Behavioral
Health Services
304 S. Main St.
Fairmont, NC 28340
910-628-6476

Mental Health Association of
Columbus County
P.O. Box 553
Whiteville, NC 28472
910-653-1414

RHA
26 Lee Ave.
Whiteville, North Carolina
910-640-2724

2. **Substance Abuse Services**
AA
Whiteville, NC 28472
910-642-4342

Community Support Agency
44 Dream Ave.
Delco, North Carolina
910-655-0698

Narcotics Anonymous
500 Jefferson St.
Whiteville, NC 28472
910-642-8011

PORT Health Services
706 N. Thompson Ave.
Whiteville, North Carolina
910-353-0109

3. **Clothing/ Food Assistance/ Financial Services**
American Red Cross
(Emergency Assistance)
704 N. Thompson St.
Whiteville, NC 28472
910-642-3364

Believers Home Fellowship-
Food Pantry
212 Faith Cir.
Tabor City, North Carolina
910-653-7299

Bogue CCA-Food Pantry
106 Jockey Rd.
Halisboro, NC 28442
910-234-5591

Columbus County
Help Mission
127 W. Commerce St.
Whiteville, NC 28472
910-642-2724

Harvest Table-Food Pantry
211 E. Columbus St.
Whiteville, NC 28472
910-642-6654

Living Word to Church-
Food Pantry
98 Old Hwy. 74
Chadbourn, NC 28431
910-654-4164

New Creations-Food Pantry
412 Youngstown Rd.
Riegelwood, NC 28456
910-669-2018

WIC Clinic
910-641-3904

4. **Housing and Shelters**
Catholic Charities
910-251-8130

Columbus County Crisis
Housing Assistance (CHAF)
111 Washington St.
Whiteville, NC 28472
910-640-1157

Columbus County
Housing Authority
50 Legion Dr., #B
Whiteville, NC 28472
910-640-6618

Families First (Shelter)
809 Washington St.
Whiteville, NC 28472
910-642-5996

Whiteville Housing Authority
504 W. Burkhead St.
Whiteville, North Carolina
910-642-4979

5. **Transportation**
Columbus
County Transportation
290 Legion Dr.
Whiteville, NC 28472
910-641-3929

6. **Medical Services**
Columbus County Community
Health Center
209 W. Virgil St.
Whiteville, NC 28472
910-641-0202

Columbus County
Health Department
304 Jefferson St.
Whiteville, NC 28472
910-640-6515

7. **Medication
Assistance Program**
Columbus County Department
of Social Services
40 Government Complex Rd.
Whiteville, NC 28472
910-642-2800

GoodRx
855-26 8-2822

Needy Meds
800-503-6897

8. **Employment/ Vocational
Rehab/ Education**
Columbus County DREAM
Center (Educational Programs)
430 S. Martin Luther King,
Jr. Avenue
Whiteville, NC 28472
910-642-0633

Department of
Vocational Rehabilitation
118 Memory Plaza
Whiteville, NC 28472
910-642-5406

Four-County Community
Services, Inc.
425 S. Lee St.
Whiteville, NC 28472
910-642-8381

JobLink Center/ ESC
630 S. Madison St.
Whiteville, NC 28472
910-642-0146

NC Works Career Center
4564 Chadbourne Hwy.
Whiteville, NC 28472
910-642-7141

9. **Legal Services**
Legal Aid of NC- (New
Hanover County)
272 N. Front St.
Wilmington, NC 28402
910-763-6207

10. **Recreational/ Leisure**
Columbus County Parks
and Recreation
106 W. Smith St.
Whiteville, NC 28472
910-640-6624

Lumber River Visitor's Center
1054 Main St.
Fair Bluff, NC 28439
910-649-7202

Nature Interpretive Center
330 Page Mill Rd.
Cerro Gordo, NC 28430
Visitor Center
301 E. 5th St.
Tabor City NC 28463
910-653-9712

11. *Special Populations*
Bolton Senior and Youth Center
15354 Sam Potts Highway
Bolton, NC 28423
910-655-4166

Boys and Girls Homes of NC,
Inc. (Child Care)
400 Flemington Dr.
Lake Waccamaw, NC 28450
910-646-3083

Bug Hill Senior Center
11300 Seven Creeks Hwy/ NC
Highway 905
Nakina, NC 28455
910-640-3791

Chadbourn Senior Center
403 Pine St.
Chadbourn, NC 28431
910-654-4423

Fair Bluff Senior Center
1100 Main St.
Fair Bluff, NC 28439
910-649-6881

East Columbus Senior Center
2694 General Howe Hwy.
Riegelwood, NC 28456
910-655-4754

Columbus County Department
of Aging/CAP Program
827 Washington St.
Whiteville, NC 28472
910-640-6602

Crisis Line (Domestic Violence)
910-641-0444

National Center for
Missing Persons
800-522-5437

Veterans Services
805 Pinckney St.
Whiteville, NC 28472
910-640-6638

CHAPTER 25

Craven County

1. **Mental Health and Crisis Services**
Crossroads Mental Health
2000 Neuse Boulevard
New Bern, NC 28560
252-633-8204

East Carolina Behavioral
Health, LME- Hertford County
144 Community College Rd.
Ahoskie, North Carolina
252-332-4137 or 252-332-5306

RHA Health Services
104 Pirates Rd.
New Bern, NC 28562
800-848-0180

2. **Substance Abuse Services**
AA
306 Avenue D
New Bern, NC 28560
252-633-3716

Coastal Coalition Substance
Abuse Program
601 Broad Street
New Bern, North Carolina
252-649-1615

Hope Recovery Homes and
Mission Ministries
3900 Bridges St.
Morehead City, North Carolina
252-515-6976

Narcotics Anonymous
866-321-1631
PORT Human Services
1309 Tatum Drive
New Bern, NC 28560
252-672-8742

3. **Clothing/ Food Assistance/ Financial Services**
Food Bank of Central and
Eastern NC
205 S. Glenburnie Rd.
New Bern, NC 28562
252-514-2006

Havelock-Cherry Point
Ministerial Association
Food Pantry
East Classic Professional Center
Suite 20
Havelock, North Carolina
252-447-5190

Religious Community Services
919 George St.
New Bern, NC 28560
252-633-2767

Salvation Army
1402 Rhem Ave.
New Bern, NC 28560
252-637-2277

The Gathering Place
114 Trader Ave.
Havelock, North Carolina
252-515-1080

WIC Program
252-636-4920

4. **Housing and Shelters**
   Coastal Women's Shelter
   1333 S. Glenburnie Rd.
   New Bern, NC 28561
   252-638-4509 or (Crisis Line)
   – 252-638-5995

   New Bern Housing Authority
   837 S. Front St.
   New Bern, NC 28562
   252-633-0800

Religious Community Services
Homeless Shelter
919 George St.
New Bern, NC 28560
252-633-2767

5. **Transportation**
   Craven Area Rural Transit
   System (CARTS)
   1106 Clarks Rd.
   New Bern, NC 28562
   252-636-4917

   New Kirk
   Transportation Services
   252-636-9070

   New Safeway Taxi
   252-636-9000

6. **Medical Services**
   Craven County Community
   Health Center
   508 US Highway 70
   Havelock, NC 28532
   252-494-1533

   Craven County
   Health Department
   2818 Neuse Blvd.
   New Bern, NC 28562
   252-636-4920

7. **Medication
   Assistance Program**
   Catholic Charities Senior
   Pharmacy Program
   252-638-2188

Craven County Department of
Social Services
2818 Neuse Blvd.
New Bern, North Carolina
252-636-4900

8. *Employment/ Vocational
Rehab/ Education*
Job Link (ESC)/NC Works
Career Center
2836 Neuse Blvd.
New Bern, NC 28562
252-514-4828

NC Division of
Vocational Rehabilitation
2832 Neuse Blvd.
New Bern, NC 28562
252-514-4727 or 877-858-8470

9. *Legal Services*
Legal Aid of NC
213 Pollock Street
New Bern, North Carolina
866-219-5262

10. *Recreational/ Leisure*
Boys and Girls Club
199 Web Blvd.
Havelock, NC 28532
252-444-5437

Boy Scouts of America
252-522-1521

Cherry Point Visitors Center
Roosevelt Blvd., Bldg #251
Marine Corps Air Station, NC
252-466-5921 or 252-466-3066

Craven County Recreation
and Parks
406 Craven St.
New Bern, NC 28560
252-636-6606

Girl Scouts
800-284-4475

New Bern Visitors Center
316 S. Front St.
New Bern, NC 28560
252-637-9400

11. *Special Populations*
City of Havelock Senior Center
103 Trader Ave.
Havelock, NC 28323
252-444-6445

Craven County Senior Services
811 George St.
New Bern, NC 28561
252-638-1790

National Child Abuse Hotline
800-422-4453

National Runaway Safeline
800-786-2929

Staff House (Pregnant Women)
252-633-4357

Veterans Services of
Craven County
2402 Dr. Martin Luther King
Junior Boulevard
New Bern, NC 28562
252-636-6611

CHAPTER 26

Cumberland County

1. ***Mental Health and Crisis Services***
Community Mental Health at Cape Fear Valley
711 Executive Pl., 3rd and 4th Floor
Fayetteville, North Carolina
910-615-3333

   Rape Crisis Center
515 Ramsey St.
Fayetteville, North Carolina
910-485-7273

   Fayetteville Veteran Center
2301 Roberson St., Suite 103
Fayetteville, North Carolina
910-488-6252 or 800-927-8387

2. ***Substance Abuse Services***
Carolina Treatment Center
3423 Melrose Rd., #A
Fayetteville, North Carolina
855-300-1544

   Celebrate Recovery (Men)
Mount Carmel Church
Fayetteville, North Carolina
910-261-6244

   Cumberland County-Crisis Detox
1724 Roxie Ave.
Fayetteville, NC 28304
910-484-1212

3. ***Clothing/ Food Assistance/ Financial Services***
Alms House
3909 Ellison St.
Hope Mills, NC 28348
910-425-0902

   Beautitude House
102 N. Main St.
Spring Lake, North Carolina
910-496-0925

   Catholic Charities
2712 Fort Bragg Rd.
Fayetteville, North Carolina
910-424-2020

Operation Blessing
(Financial Assistance)
1337 Ramsey St.
Fayetteville, NC 28301
910-483-1119

Second Harvest Food Bank
406 Deep Creek Rd.
Fayetteville, North Carolina
910-485-6923

Seth's Wish
330 S. Cool Springs St.
Fayetteville, North Carolina
910-476-6613

The Church of Cedar Creek
(Food)
4010 Cedar Creek Rd.
Fayetteville, North Carolina
910-483-6895

WIC Clinic
910-321-6420 (Spring Lake)
910-433-3760 or 910-433-3730
(Fayetteville)

4. **Housing and Shelters**
Care Center Transitional
Housing (Domestic
Violence-Women)
245 Alexander St.
Fayetteville, North Carolina
910-485-8026

City Rescue Mission
120 N. Cool Springs St.
Fayetteville, North Carolina
910-323-0446

Fayetteville Metropolitan
Housing Authority
1000 Ramsey St.
Fayetteville, NC 28301
910-483-3648

Green's Shelter for Women
333 Hawley Road
Fayetteville, North Carolina
910-717-7009

Hope Center (Women)
913 Person St.
Fayetteville, North Carolina
910-364-2981

New Life Mission (Men)
910-864-4678
Oxford House
511 Spruce Dr.
Fayetteville, North Carolina
910-568-3698 (Men)
910-491-3271 (Women)

Salvation Army
(Emergency Shelter)
22 E. Russell St.
Fayetteville, NC 28301
910-483-8119, extension 242

5. **Transportation**
Community
Transportation Program of
Cumberland County
130 Gillespie Street
Fayetteville, North Carolina
910-678-7619

Fayetteville Area System of
Transit (FAST)
455 Grove St.
Fayetteville, NC 28301
910-433-1747 or 910-433-1232
(ADA)

Fayetteville Regional Airport
400 Airport Rd., Suite 101
Fayetteville, NC 28306
910-433-1160

Homeless Project Office
(Bus Passes)
Fayetteville City Police
910-433-1846

6. Medical Services
Care Clinic
239 Robeson St.
Fayetteville, NC 28301
910-485-0555

Fayetteville County
Health Department
1235 Ramsey St.
Fayetteville, NC 28301
910-433-3600

Goshen Medical Center
3613 Cape Center Dr.
Fayetteville, North Carolina
910-354-1720

VA Hospital
2300 Ramsey Street,
Building 50
Fayetteville, North Carolina
910-488-2120, x7744 or
800-771-6106

7. Medication Assistance Program
Cumberland County
Department of Social Services
1225 Ramsey St.
Fayetteville, North Carolina
910-677-2392 or 910-323-1540

Cumberland County Health
Department-Medicaid
Access Program
1235 Ramsey St., 1st Floor
Fayetteville, North Carolina
910-433-3739

Prescription Discount Cards
877-321-2652

8. Employment/ Vocational Rehab/ Education
Action Pathways
321 Dick St.
Fayetteville, North Carolina
910-223-0116

Department of
Vocational Rehabilitation
1200 Fairmont Ct.
Fayetteville, North Carolina
910-486-1101 or 910-486-1548

NC Works Career Center
414 Ray Ave.
Fayetteville, North Carolina
910-486-1010 or 910-323-3421

9. Legal Services
Legal Aid of NC
327 Dick St., Suite 103
Fayetteville, North Carolina
910-483-0400 or 800-824-5340

10. *Recreational/ Leisure*

Fort Liberty Visitor Center
3500 All-American Freeway
Fort Liberty (prev. Fort Bragg),
NC 28310
910-907-5165

Visitor Center-
Distinctly Fayetteville
245 Person St.
Fayetteville, NC 28301
910-483-5311
Welcome Center
Lowdermilk Drive
Fayetteville, NC 28311

11. *Special Populations*

Army Community Service
Family Advocacy Program
(Domestic Violence)
Soldier Support Center,
Building 4-2843, 3rd Floor
Normandy Drive
Fort Liberty, North Carolina
910-396-5521

CELL Phones for Low-Income/
Homeless
800-723-3546 Safe Link

888-898-4888
Assurance Wireless
Cumberland County
Veterans Services
301 E. Russell St.
Fayetteville, North Carolina
910-677-2970

Fayetteville Dream Center
(Diaper Bank)
336 Ray Ave.
Fayetteville, North Carolina
910-568-3897

Fayetteville Senior Center
739 Blue St.
Fayetteville, North Carolina
910-433-1574

CHAPTER 27

Currituck County

1. **Mental Health and Crisis Services**
Albemarle Mental Health Center-Pasquotank County
Elizabeth City, North Carolina
252-338-8352

Trillium Health Resources-Craven County
800 Cardinal Rd.
New Bern, NC 28563
877-685-2415

2. **Substance Abuse Services**
AA Hotline
800-350-2538

Mental Health/Substance Abuse Program
Currituck County,
North Carolina
252-453-8886

3. **Clothing/ Food Assistance/ Financial Services**
Brother's Keeper Thrift Store
3935 Caratoke Highway
Barco, NC 27917
252-435-3873

Community Action
P.O. Box 189
Currituck, NC 27929
252-232-2882

Food Bank, Emergency Food Center
PO Box 65
Currituck, NC 27929
252-232-2324

It's All Good Thrift and Gift
9138 Caratoke Highway
Point Harbor, NC 27964
252-207-7468

WIC Clinic
252-232-2271

4. **Housing and Shelters**
Albemarle Hopeline
(Domestic Violence Shelter)-
Pasquotank County
Elizabeth's City, North Carolina
252-338-3011

Catholic Charities (Assistance)
252-426-7717

5. **Transportation**
Currituck County Department
of Social Services
2793 Caratoke Highway
Currituck, NC 27929
252-232-3083

6. **Medical Services**
Currituck County
Health Department
2795 Caratoke Highway
Currituck, NC 27929
252-232-2271

7. **Medication
Assistance Program**
Currituck County Department
of Social Services
2793 Caratoke Highway
Currituck, NC 27929
252-232-3083

Rx Outreach
P.O. Box 66536
St. Louis, MO 63166
888-796-1234

8. **Employment/ Vocational
Rehab/ Education**
Currituck County Job
Link Center
P.O. Box 99
Currituck, NC 27929
252-232-3083

NC Works Career Center-
Dare County
2522 S. Croatan Highway
Nags Head, NC 27959
252-480-3500

9. **Legal Services**
Legal Services of the Coastal
Plains-Hertford County
610 E. Church St.
Ahoskie, NC 27910
919-332-5124 or 800-682-0010

10. **Recreational/ Leisure**
Currituck Outer Banks
Visitor's Center
106 Caratoke Highway
Moyock, NC 27958
252-435-2947

11. **Special Populations**
Currituck County
Senior Center
130 Community Way
Barco, NC 27917
252-232-3505

Currituck County
Senior Center
2793 Caratoke Highway
Currituck, NC 27929
252-232-3505

Knotts Island Senior Center
126 Brumley Rd.
Knotts Island NC 27950
252-429-3231

Powells Point Senior Center
8011 Character Hwy.
Powells Point, NC 27966
252-491-8173

Veterans Services-
Pasquotank County
1023 US Highway 17, South
Elizabeth City, NC 27909
252-331-4741

CHAPTER 28

Dare County

1. ***Mental Health and Crisis Services***
Outer Banks Crisis Hotline, Inc.
Amadas Street-Highway 602
Manteo, NC 27954
252-473-5121

2. ***Substance Abuse Services***
Faith by the Sea-Kitty Hawk
800-519-2977

   Footprints in Recovery – Kill Devil Hills
877-429-0713

   Kitty Hawk Alcohol Addiction Treatment Program
888-439-3435

   PORT/New Horizons (Outpatient Treatment)
2808 S. Croatan Highway, Suite B
Nags Head, NC 27959
252-441-2324

   Rite Path Addiction Treatment and Counseling
106 W. Woodhill Dr.
Nags Head, NC 27959
252-986-3100

3. ***Clothing/ Food Assistance/ Financial Services***
Beach Food Pantry
4007 N. Croatan Highway
Kitty Hawk, NC 27949
252-261-2756

   Interfaith Community Outreach
115 Mustian Street
Kill Devil Hills, NC 27948
252-480-0070

   Room in the Inn
252-255-1133

   Ruthie's Community Kitchen
1311 Goldie St.
Nags Head, NC 27948
252-207-8820

WIC Clinic
252-475-5068

4. **Housing and Shelters**
Battered Women's
Shelter-Manteo
252-473-5121

OBX (Men)
302 Gunas Dr.
Kill Devil Hills, NC 27948
252-715-3786

Ocean Acres (Men)
305 W. Ocean Acres Drive
Kill Devil Hills, NC 27948
252-715-1272

Outer Banks Relief Foundation
103 E. 8th St.
Nags Head, NC 27959
252-261-2004

Shelter/Housing Bay (Men)
1201 7th Ave.
Kill Devil Hills, NC 27948
252-715-4393

5. **Transportation**
Dare County
Transportation System
954 Marshall C. Collins Drive,
Room 181
Manteo, NC 27954
252-475-5640 or 252-475-5003

6. **Medical Services**
Community Care Clinic
of Dare
425 Health Center Dr.
Nags Head, NC 27959
252-261-3041

Dare County
Health Department
109 Exeter St.
Manteo, NC 27954
252-473-1101

Dare County Health
Department-Buxton
Highway 12 and Buxton
Back Road
Buxton, NC 27920
252-995-4404

7. **Medication
Assistance Program**
Dare County Department of
Social Services
P.O. Box 859
Buxton, NC 27920
252-995-4404

Dare County Department of
Social Services
107 Exeter St.
Manteo, NC 27954
252-473-1471

Rx Outreach
PO Box 66536
St. Louis, MO 63166
888-796-1234

8. ***Employment/ Vocational Rehab/ Education***
Job Link Center-ESC/NC Works Career Center
2522 S. Croatan Highway
MP 13, Box 757
Nags Head, NC 27959
252-480-3500

Vocational Rehabilitation-Pasquotank County
252-331-4768

9. ***Legal Services***
Legal Services of the Coastal Plains-Hertford County
610 Church St., East
Ahoskie, NC 27910
800-682-0010 or 866-219-5262

10. ***Recreational/ Leisure***
Dare County Parks and Recreation
46380 Highway 12
Buxton, NC 27920
252-475-5650

Dare County Parks and Recreation
602 Mustian St.
Kill Devil Hills, NC 27948
252-475-5920

Dare County Parks and Recreation
1000 Wescott Park Rd.
Manteo, NC 27954
252-475-5910

Outer Banks Visitor Center
1 Visitors Center Circle
Manteo, NC 27954
877-629-4386

11. ***Special Populations***
Baum Seniors Center
300 Mustian Street
Kill Devil Hills, NC 27948
252-441-1181 or 252-475-5635 (Baum)
252-475-9320 (Frisco)
252-475-5500 (Manteo)

Veterans Services Office
204 Ananias Dare Street
Manteo, North Carolina
252-475-5604

CHAPTER 29

Davidson County

1. ***Mental Health and Crisis Services***
CareNet Counseling
250 Hospital Dr., Room #414
Lexington, North Carolina
336-238-4763

   Davidson County
Mental Health
203 Lexington Ave.
Lexington, NC 27295
336-474-2700

2. ***Substance Abuse Services***
DayMark Recovery
Services, Inc.
1104-A S. Main St.
Lexington, NC 27292
336-242-2450

3. ***Clothing/ Food Assistance/ Financial Services***
Davidson Community Action
15 E. 2nd Ave.
Lexington, NC 27292
336-249-0234

   Salvation Army (Soup Kitchen)
314 W. 9th Ave.
Lexington, NC 27292
336-481-7324

   West Davidson Food Pantry
4600 W. Old Hwy. 64
Lexington, NC 27295
336-787-4357

4. ***Housing and Shelters***
Lexington Housing Authority
(Eastview Terrace)
1 Jamaica Dr.
Lexington, North Carolina
336-249-8936

   Thomasville Housing
201 James Ave.
Thomasville, North Carolina
336-475-6137

5. ***Transportation***
Department of Transportation
945 N. Main St.
Lexington, NC 27292
336-883-7278

6. **Medical Services**
   Davidson County
   Health Department
   913 Greensboro St.
   Lexington, NC 27292
   336-242-2210

7. **Medication
   Assistance Program**
   Davidson County Department
   of Social Services
   913 Greensboro St.
   Lexington, NC 27292
   336-242-2500

8. **Employment/ Vocational
   Rehab/ Education**
   Davidson Works
   220 E. 1st Ave., Extension
   Lexington, NC 27292
   336-242-2065

9. **Legal Services**
   Legal Services-
   Mecklenburg County
   1431 Elizabeth Ave.
   Charlotte, NC 28204
   704-376-1600

10. **Recreational/ Leisure**
    Lexington Visitor Center
    2 N. Main St.
    Lexington, NC 27292
    336-236-4218

11. **Special Populations**
    Alcoholics Anonymous (AA)
    336-249-6636

    Family Services
    (Domestic Violence)
    336-243-1934

    Senior Services
    555-B W. Center St., Extension
    Lexington, NC 27295
    336-242-2290

    Veterans Services
    913 Greensboro St., Suite 101
    Lexington, NC 27292
    336-242-2037

CHAPTER 30

Davie County

1. **Mental Health and Crisis Services**
Behavioral Health (DCHHS)
172 S. Clement St.
Mocksville, NC 27028
336-753-6440

Davie Medical Center
(CareNet)
329 NC Highway 801 N.
Bermuda Run, NC 27006
336-716-0855

HELP (Domestic Violence)
336-751-4357

2. **Substance Abuse Services**
DayMark Recovery Services
377 Hospital St., Suite 100
Mocksville, NC 27028
336-751-5636

3. **Clothing/ Food Assistance/ Financial Services**
Cooleemee Community
Food Pantry
204 Marginal St.
Cooleemee, NC 27014
336-284-2626

Just HOPE, Inc.
643 Wilkesboro St.
Mocksville, NC 27028
336-909-4241

4. **Housing and Shelters**
Housing Department
123 S. Main St.
Mocksville, NC 27028
336-753-6100

5. **Transportation**
Transportation (Parks & Rec.)
644 N. Main St.
Mocksville, NC 27028
336-753-8326

YVEDDI
336-367-7251

6. ***Medical Services***
   Davie County
   Health Department
   154 Government Center Dr.
   Mocksville, NC 27028
   336-753-6750

7. ***Medication***
   Assistance Program
   Davie County Department of
   Social Services
   154 Government Center Dr.
   Mocksville, NC 27028
   336-753-6250

8. ***Employment/ Vocational***
   Rehab/ Education
   North Carolina Vocational
   Rehabilitation Services
   375 Hospital St., Suite 100
   Mocksville, NC 27028
   336-936-6150

9. ***Legal Services***
   Legal Aid-Forsyth County
   102 W. 3rd St., Suite 460
   Winston-Salem, NC 27101
   336-75-9162 or 800-660-6663

10. ***Recreational/ Leisure***
    Davie County Visitors Center
    135 S. Salisbury St.
    Mocksville, NC 27028
    336-751-3304

11. ***Special Populations***
    Davie County Senior Services
    278 Meroney St.
    Mocksville, NC 27028
    336-753-6230

    Veteran's Administration
    140 S. Main St.
    Mocksville, NC 27028
    336-751-2010 or 336-753-6015

CHAPTER 31

Duplin County

1. **Mental Health and Crisis Services**
East Carolina Behavioral Health
877-685-2415

New Dimension Group
416 W. Ridge St.
Rose Hill, NC 28458
910-289-2610

Vidant Psychiatric Program
Vidant General Hospital
401 N. Main St.
Kenansville, NC 28349
910-296-2787

2. **Substance Abuse Services**
Al-Anon
Kenansville Baptist Church
122 Routledge Road
Kenansville, NC 28349
Alcohol and Drug Abuse
Helpline and Treatment
800-331-2900

Eastpointe Human Services
514 E. Main St.
Beulaville, NC 28518
800-913-6109

Narcotics Anonymous (NA)
United Methodist Church
110 E. Bridger St.
Burgaw, NC 28425
800-591-6474

3. **Clothing/ Food Assistance/ Financial Services**
Eastern Baptist Association
(Food Pantry)
109 N. Center St.
Warsaw, NC 28398

Food Pantry-Wallace Church
of God
1173 Bay Rd.
Teachey, NC 28464
910-285-2394

New Elders Chapel Food Pantry
1555 NC 11 Highway
Magnolia, NC 28453
910-285-5032

The Sanctuary Project
(Food Assistance)
121 W. Main St.
Wallace, NC 28466
910-518-1255

WIC Clinic
910-296-2130

4. Housing and Shelters
Duplin County Housing
421 N. Pine St.
Rose Hill, North Carolina
910-289-3985

Eastern Carolina Regional
Housing Authority
Beulaville, North Carolina
910-289-3377

Eastern Carolina Regional
Housing Authority
Magnolia, North Carolina
910-289-2750

Oxford House-Archway East
(Shelter)
P.O. Box 39
Rose Hill, NC 28458
910-289-2342

Sarah's Refuge
(Domestic Violence)
106 N. Front St.
Warsaw, NC 28398
910-293-3467

5. Transportation
Duplin County
Transportation Department
209 Seminary St.
Kenansville, NC 28349
910-296-2333

6. Medical Services
Goshen Medical Center
444 SW Center Street
Faison, NC 28341
910-267-0421

**7. Medication
Assistance Program**
Duplin County Department of
Social Services
423 N. Main St.
Kenansville, NC 28349
910-296-2200

GoodRx
855-268-2822

Rx Outreach
888-796-1234

Seniors Health Insurance
Information Program (SHIP)
855-408-1212

**8. Employment/ Vocational
Rehab/ Education**
Duplin County Vocational
Rehabilitation Services
103 W. Hill St.
Kenansville, NC 28398
910-296-0049

Eastern Carolina Human
Services Agency
208 W. Railroad St.
Wallace, NC 28466
910-285-7077

NC Works Career Center/
JobLink
192 Magnolia Extension
Kenansville, NC 28349
910-296-1472

9. **Legal Services**

Legal Aid-New
Hanover County
272 N. Front St.
Wilmington, NC 28401
910-763-6207

10. **Recreational/ Leisure**

Cabin Lake/Duplin County
Parks and Recreation
224 Seminary St.
Kenansville, NC 28349
910-296-2104

Kenansville Parks
and Recreation
501 S. Main St.
Kenansville, NC 28349
910-290-1579

Duplin County Tourism Office
195 Fairgrounds Drive
Kenansville, NC 28349
910-296-2181

11. **Special Populations**

Boys Town Crisis and
Suicide Hotline
800-448-3000 or 800-448-1833

Duplin County Senior Center
213 Seminary St.
Kenansville, NC 28349
910-296-2140

Duplin County
Veteran Services
160 Mallard St.
Kenansville, NC 28349
910-296-2114

National Domestic
Violence Hotline
800-799-SAFE (7233)

National Sexual Assault Hotline
800-656-HOPE

CHAPTER 32

Durham County

1. **Mental Health and Crisis Services**
Center for Child &
Family Health
1121 W. Chapel Hill St.,
Suite 100
Durham, NC 27701
919-419-3474

Healing with CAARE, Inc.
214 Broadway St.
Durham, NC 27701
919-683-5300

2. **Substance Abuse Services**
Durham Recovery
Response Center
309 Crutchfield St.
Durham, NC 27704
919-560-7305

RJ Blackley Alcohol & Drug
Abuse Treatment Center
919-575-7928

3. **Clothing/ Food Assistance/ Financial Services**
American Red Cross
4737 University Dr.
Durham, NC 27707
919-489-6541

Dress for Success
919-286-2128

Food Pantry
410 Liberty St.
Durham, NC 27701
919-682-0583

The Giving Closet
721 Foster St.
Durham, NC 27701
919-560-7150

Meals on Wheels
919-667-9424

Rougemont Community
Food Pantry
United Methodist Church
105 Red Mountain Rd.
Rougemont, NC 27572
919-245-0015

Salvation Army
919 Liberty St.
Durham, NC 27702
919-688-7306

4. **Housing and Shelters**
Durham Housing Authority
330 E. Main St.
Durham, North Carolina
919-683-1511

Durham Rescue Mission
1201 E. Main St.
Durham, NC 27701
919-688-9641

Open Table
919-412-7011

5. **Transportation**
Go Durham
515 W. Pettigrew St.
Durham, NC 27701
919-485-7433

Go Durham Access
1911 Fay Street
Durham, NC 27701
919-560-1511

6. **Medical Services**
Durham County
Health Department
414 E. Main St.
Durham, North Carolina
919-560-7650

Lincoln Community
Health Center
130 Fayetteville St.
Durham, NC 27707
919-956-4000

7. **Medication
Assistance Program**
Durham County Department of
Social Services
414 E. Main St.
Durham, NC 27701
919560-8600

8. **Employment/ Vocational
Rehab/ Education**
NC Works
1105 S. Briggs Ave.
Durham, NC 27703
919-560-6880

Vocational Rehabilitation
4312 Western Park Pl.
Durham, North Carolina
919-560-6810

9. **Legal Services**
Legal Aid of NC
201 W. Main St., Suite 400
Durham, North Carolina
919-688-6396

10. *Recreational/ Leisure*
Durham Visitor Info Center
212 W. Main St., #101
Durham, NC 27701
919-687-0288

11. *Special Populations*
Alliance of all AIDS Services
919-596-9898

Durham Center for Senior Life
Henderson Towers
807 S. Duke St.
Durham, North Carolina
919-688-8247

Durham Crisis Response
Center (Domestic Violence)
919-403-6562

Durham Veteran
Services Officer
200 N. Mangum St.
Durham, North Carolina
919-560-8387

Rights of Passage Program
(African American boys)
908 Fayetteville St., Suite 202
Durham, NC 27701
919-683-1047

CHAPTER 33

Edgecombe County

1. *Mental Health and Crisis Services*
Edge-Nash Mental Health
Service / Eastpointe
500 Nash Medical Arts Mall
Rocky Mount, NC 27804
252-937-8141 or 888-893-8640

Monarch Behavioral Health-
Crisis Services
809 Tiffany Blvd.
Rocky Mount, NC 27804
252-442-0333

NEED, Inc. (Referral Service)
200 N. Church St.
Rocky Mount, NC 27804
252-442-8081

2. *Substance Abuse Services*
New Horizons
(Narcotics Anonymous)
877-590-6262

Oxford House (Men)
519 Hammond St.
Rocky Mount, North Carolina
252-442-6566

Oxford House (Women)
1333 Hill St.
Rocky Mount, North Carolina
252-407-7968

PORT Human Services-
Pitt County
114 E. 3rd St.
Greenville, NC 27858
252-752-2431

The Lighthouse
1016 Eastern Ave.
Rocky Mount, North Carolina
252-314-0975

3. *Clothing/ Food Assistance/ Financial Services*
A Touch of the Father's Love
Ministry (Food Pantry)
200 W. Battleboro Ave.
Battleboro, NC 27809
252-377-2209

Community
Enrichment Organization
403 Beasley St.
Tarboro, NC 27886
252-641-1733

Meals on Wheels
1501 Sunset Ave.
Rocky Mount, North Carolina
252-446-4336

Peacemakers Family Center
1725 Davis St.
Rocky Mount, North Carolina
252-972-7473

Regeneration Development
Group (Food Pantry)
107 NE 1st St.
Pinetops, NC 27864
252-827-1800

Salvation Army
420 Paul St.
Rocky Mount, NC 27803
252-446-4496

WIC Clinic
252-985-1067

4. Housing and Shelters
My Sister's House (Women of
Domestic Violence)
Rocky Mount, North Carolina
252-462-0366

Princeville Housing Authority
Princeville, North Carolina
252-823-3889

Rocky Mount
Housing Authority
1006 Aycock St.
Rocky Mount, North Carolina
252-977-3141

Tarboro Community Outreach
(Shelter)
701 Cedar Ln.
Barbara, NC 27886
252-823-8801

Tarboro Housing Authority
947 Simmons St.
Tarboro, North Carolina
252-823-6339

The Bassett Center Shelter
(Families with Children)
916 Branch St.
Rocky Mount, North Carolina
252-985-0078

5. Transportation
Tar River Transit
100 Coastline St., Suite 315
Rocky Mount, NC 27804
252-972-1174

6. Medical Services
Carolina Family Health Center
162 Highway 33, East
Princeville, North Carolina
252-641-0514

Edgecombe County
Health Department
155 Atlantic Ave.
Rocky Mount, NC 27801
252-985-4100

Edgecombe County
Health Department
122 E. St. James Street
Tarboro, NC 27886
252-641-7511

Vidant Edgecombe Hospital
111 Hospital Dr.
Tarboro, NC 27886
252-641-7700

7. *Medication
Assistance Program*
Edgecombe County
Department of Social
Services-Tarboro
122 E. St. James Street
Tarboro, NC 27886
252-641-7835

Edgecombe County
Department of Social Services
301 S. Fairview Rd.
Rocky Mount, NC 27801
252-985-4101

GoodRx
855-268-2822

8. *Employment/ Vocational
Rehab/ Education*
NC Works Career Center
110 Fountain Park Dr.
Rocky Mount, NC 27803
252-977-3306

SWIM Network, Inc.
252-266-2291

Vocational
Rehabilitation Division
201 Saint Andrew St.
Tarboro, NC 27886
252-641-7849

9. *Legal Services*
Eastern Carolina Legal Services
148 S. Washington St.
Rocky Mount, NC 27804
252-442-0635 or 866-219-5262

Legal Aid of
NC-Wilson County
208 Goldsboro St.
Wilson, North Carolina
800-682-7902

10. *Recreational/ Leisure*
Town of Tarboro
Recreation Department
1501 Western Blvd.
Tarboro, NC 27886
252-641-4210

YMCA
1000 Independence Dr.
Rocky Mount, NC 27804
252-972-9622

11. *Special Populations*
Center on Aging
201 Saint Andrew St.,
Room 264
Tarboro, NC 27886
252-641-5831

National Call Center for
Homeless Vets
877-424-3838

Rocky Mount-Edgecombe CDC
148 S. Washington St.
Rocky Mount, North Carolina
252-442-5178

Veterans Services Office
County
Administration Building
201 Saint Andrews St.
Tarboro, NC 27886
252-641-7846

CHAPTER 34

Forsyth County

1. **Mental Health and Crisis Services**
Mental Health Association in Forsyth County
1509 S. Hawthorne Rd.
Winston-Salem, North Carolina
336-768-3880

   Monarch
4140 N. Cherry St.
Winston-Salem, North Carolina
866-272-7826

   Old Vineyard Behavioral Health Services
3637 Old Vineyard Rd.
Winston-Salem, North Carolina
336-794-3550

2. **Substance Abuse Services**
Alcoholics Anonymous
2569 Reynolda Rd.
Winston-Salem, North Carolina
336-723-1452

   Burgess Wellness
1951 N. Peacehaven Rd.
Winston-Salem, North Carolina
336-900-5595

   DayMark Recovery Services
20 W. 32nd St.
Winston-Salem, North Carolina
336-722-4000

3. **Clothing/ Food Assistance/ Financial Services**
Catholic Charities
Diocese Pantry
1612 E. 14th St.
Winston-Salem, NC 27105
336-727-0705

   Clemmons Food Pantry
2585 Old Glory Rd.
Clemmons, NC 27012
336-331-3432

   Crisis Control Ministry
(Food Pantry)
431 W. Bodenhamer St.
Kernersville, NC 27284
336-996-5401

Dress for Success
375 Buxton St.
Winston-Salem, North Carolina
336-970-0374

Financial Pathways of
the Piedmont
7820 N. Point Blvd., Suite 100
Winston-Salem, North Carolina
336-896-1191

Morris Chapel United
Methodist Church Pantry
2715 Darrow Rd.
Walkertown, NC 27051
336-595-8101

Salvation Army
901 Cleveland Ave.
Winston-Salem, NC 27101
336-722-8721

Samaritan Ministries
1243 Patterson Ave.
Winston-Salem, North Carolina
336-748-1962

WIC Clinic
336-703-3336

4. **Housing and Shelters**
Bethesda Center (Shelter)
930 N. Patterson Ave.
Winston-Salem, North Carolina
336-722-9951

Salvation Army
1255 N. Trade St.
Winston-Salem, North Carolina
336-722-8721

Winston-Salem
Housing Authority
901 Cleveland Ave.
Winston-Salem, North Carolina
336-727-8500

Winston-Salem Rescue Mission
(Shelter)
717 Oak St.
Winston-Salem, North Carolina
336-723-1848

5. **Transportation**
Allegiance
Transportation Services
100 W. 5th St.
Winston-Salem, North Carolina
336-962-7433

Piedmont Authority for
Regional Transportation
(PART)
336-883-7278

Safe Ride Transportation
336-995-7529

Winston-Salem
Transit Authority
100 W. 5th St.
Winston-Salem, North Carolina
336-727-2000

6. **Medical Services**
Forsyth County
Health Department
799 Highland Ave.
Winston-Salem, NC 27102
336-703-3100

7. ***Medication Assistance Program***
Forsyth County Department of Social Services
741 N. Highland Ave.
Winston-Salem, NC 27101
336-703-3400 or 336-703-3800

NC Med Assistance
704-536-1790

8. ***Employment/ Vocational Rehab/ Education***
Job Corps Scholars Program
Winston-Salem State University
601 S. Martin Luther King, Jr. Drive
Winston-Salem, North Carolina
336-750-2000

NC Division of Vocational Rehabilitation Services
2201 Brewer Rd.
Winston-Salem, North Carolina
336-968-3230

NC Works Career Center of Forsyth County
2701 University Pkwy.
Winston-Salem, North Carolina
336-464-0520

9. ***Legal Services***
Legal Aid
216 W. 4th St.
Winston-Salem, North Carolina
336-75-9166 or 336-75-9162

Legal Aid of NC
102 W. 3rd St., #460
Winston-Salem, North Carolina
866-219-5262

10. ***Recreational/ Leisure***
Winston-Salem Tourist Information Center
200 Brookstown Ave.
Winston-Salem, NC 27101
336-728-4200

11. ***Special Populations***
Family Services
(Domestic Violence)
610 Coliseum Dr.
Winston-Salem, North Carolina
336-722-8173 or (Crisis Line)
336-723-4457

Senior Services, Inc.
2895 Shorefair Dr.
Winston-Salem, NC 27105
336-725-0907

Walnut Cove Senior Citizens Center
336-591-5442

CHAPTER 35

Franklin County

1. **Mental Health and Crisis Services**
Cardinal Innovation Healthcare Solutions-Vance County
134 S. Garnet St.
Henderson, NC 27536
252-430-1330

Central Community Services
919-496-3958

Five County MH/DD/SA-Halifax County-Halifax County
210 Smith Church Road
Roanoke Rapids, North Carolina
252-537-6174

Mental Health/Substance Abuse Program
Franklin County, North Carolina
919-496-4111

Recovery Response Center-Vance County
300 Park View Dr., West
Henderson, NC 27536
252-438-4145

2. **Substance Abuse Services**
Addiction Recovery Center for Men-Vance County
1020 County Home Rd.
Henderson, NC 27536
252-492-5746

Alcohol/Drug Council of NC
800-688-4232

Quitline NC
800-QUIT-NOW
Vaya Health
800-939-5911

Vision Behavioral Health Services
104 N. Main St., Suite 200
Louisburg, NC 27549
919-496-7781

3. **Clothing/ Food Assistance/ Financial Services**
GCF Donation Center and Store (Clothes)
136 S. Bickett Blvd.
Louisburg, NC 27549
919-340-1181

Life Line Outreach Inc. (Food)- Vance County
2014 Raleigh Rd.
Henderson, NC 27536
252-438-2098

4. **Housing and Shelters**
Area Christians Together in Service (ACTS)-Domestic Violence Shelter
201 S. William St.
Henderson, NC 27536
252-492-8231

Care and Share (Shelter)- Vance County
P.O. Box 116
Henderson, NC 27536
252-492-5746

Housing Services Department/ F-V-W Opportunity Inc.
167 Highway 56 E.
Louisburg, NC 27549
919-496-3022

Safe Space, Inc. (Shelter)
304 E. Nash St.
Louisburg, NC 27549
919-497-5444

5. **Transportation**
Kerr Area Rural Travel Transportation (KARTS)
1575 Ross Mill Rd.
Henderson, NC 27537
252-438-2573

6. **Medical Services**
Advanced Community Health
919-833-3111

Bunn Medical Center
919-496-2889

Franklin County Health Department
107 Industrial Dr., Suite C
Louisburg, NC 27549
919-496-8110

STD Hotline
800-227-8922

Youngsville Chiropractor Center
919-556-2001

7. **Medication Assistance Program**
Franklin County Department of Social Services
107 Industrial Dr., #A
Louisburg, NC 27549
919-496-5721

8. **Employment/ Vocational Rehab/ Education**
Franklin County JobLink Centers/Employment Security Commission
90 Tanglewood Dr.
Louisburg, NC 27549
919-496-6477

Franklin County Workforce Center
6 N. Main St.
Franklinton, NC 27525
919-494-1162

Vocational Rehabilitation
599 S. Bickett Blvd.
Louisburg, North Carolina
919-496-3124

9. **Legal Services**
Legal Aid of NC-Durham County
201 W. Main St., Suite 400
Durham, NC 27702
919-688-6396

10. **Recreational/ Leisure**
Franklin County Parks and Recreation
919-496-6624

Franklin County Tourism Development Authority
112 E. Nash St.
Louisburg, NC 27549
919-496-3056

11. **Special Populations**
Americans with Disabilities Act Hotline
800-514-0301

Franklin County Veteran Services Officer
S. Main St.- Courthouse Annex
Louisburg, North Carolina
919-496-1939

Franklinton Senior Center
919-494-5611

Louisburg Senior Center
167 NC 56 Highway
Louisburg, NC 27549
919-496-1131

NC Poison Control
800-222-1222

CHAPTER 36

Gaston County

1. Mental Health and Crisis Services
National Suicide
Prevention Lifeline
800-273-8255

The Arc
200 E. Franklin Blvd.
Gastonia, North Carolina
704-861-1036

2. Substance Abuse Services
Alcoholics Anonymous (AA)
704-865-1561

National Help Line for
Substance Abuse
800-262-2463

Pathways
2505 Court Dr.
Gastonia, North Carolina
704-854-4204

3. Clothing/ Food Assistance/ Financial Services
Belmont
Community Organization
91 E. Catawba Street
Belmont, NC 28012
704-629-2147

American Red Cross-Gaston
County Chapter
190 S. Oakland St.
Gastonia, North Carolina
704-864-2623

4. Housing and Shelters
Salvation Army
107 S. Broad Street
Gastonia, North Carolina
704-867-6145

The Shelter of Gaston County
330 N. Marietta St.
Gastonia, North Carolina
704-852-6000

Belmont Housing Authority
704-825-9376

Gastonia Housing Authority
704-864-6771

Mount Holly
Housing Authority
704-827-9025

5. **Transportation**
Gaston County Department of
Social Services
330 N. Marietta St.
Gastonia, NC 28052
704-862-7500

6. **Medical Services**
Gaston County
Health Department
991 Hudson Blvd.
Gastonia, North Carolina
704-853-5000

Gaston Family Health Services
991 Hudson Blvd.
Gastonia, North Carolina
704-853-5079

Helping Hands Free Clinic
105 Dave Warlick Drive
Lincolnton, North Carolina
704-735-7145

Dental Clinic
704-853-5191

7. **Medication
Assistance Program**
Gaston County Department of
Social Services
330 N. Marietta St.
Gastonia, NC 28052
704-862-7500

8. **Employment/ Vocational
Rehab/ Education**
Vocational Rehabilitation
109 W. 8th Ave.
Gastonia, NC 28054
704-853-5358 or 877-282-0757

9. **Legal Services**
Gaston County Magistrate
704-852-3310

Gaston County Police
Victim Assistance
704-866-3320

NC Victim Assistance Network
800-348-5068

10. **Recreational/ Leisure**
Gaston Boys and Girls Club
310 S. Boyd St.
Gastonia, North Carolina
704-810-9524

Gaston County Center of
Tourism Development
620 N. Main St.
Belmont, NC 28012
704-825-4044

11. **Special Populations**
AVID (Domestic Violence)
Crisis Line 704-864-0060

Gaston County Senior Center
1303 Dallas Cherryville Hwy.
Dallas, NC 28034
704-922-2170

Gaston County Department of
Veterans Services
955 Roberts Dr.
Gastonia, NC 28054
704-866-3606

House of Mercy (HIV/AIDS)
21 McCauley Drive
Belmont, NC 28012
704-825-8832

National Domestic
Violence Hotline
800-799-SAFE (7233)

CHAPTER 37

Gates County

1. ***Mental Health and Crisis Services***
Crisis Center (Referral Service)
877-685-2420

Integrated Family Services-
Hertford County
312 S. Academy St., Suite B
Ahoskie, NC 27910
252-209-0388 or 866-437-1821

Mental Health/Substance
Abuse Program
Gates County, North Carolina
252-357-1380

Trillium Health Resources
Crisis Services
877-685-2415

2. ***Substance Abuse Services***
AA
252-338-1849 or 800-350-2538

Narcotics Anonymous
888-370-6262

Port Human Services-
Pitt County
4300 Sapphire Ct., #110
Greenville, North Carolina
252-830-7540

3. ***Clothing/ Food Assistance/ Financial Services***
Ballard's Grove Baptist Church
730 NC Highway 137
Eure, NC 27935
252-642-4070

Damascus Road
Worship Center
739 NC Highway 137
Eure, NC 27935
252-357-0321

Food Pantry of
Washington County
811 Washington St.
Plymouth, North Carolina
252-793-4152

Gates Emergency Ministries
(GEMS)-Food Pantry
252 NC Highway 37, North
Gatesville, NC 27937
252-337-6599

WIC Clinic
252-357-1380

4. **Housing and Shelters**
Catholic Charities
(Housing Assistance)
252-426-7717

Salvation Army (Housing
Assistance)-Pasquotank County
602 N. Hughes Blvd.
Elizabeth City, NC 27909
252-338-4129

The Arc of NC (Group Homes
for Disabled)
Eure, North Carolina
919-577-5023

The Garden of Hope
House (Women Shelter)-
Pasquotank County
508 S. Road St.
Elizabeth City, NC 27909
252-335-0080

5. **Transportation**
Gates County Inter-Regional
Transportation System (GITS)
714 Main St.
Gatesville, NC 27938
252-357-4487

Human Service Transportation
Gatesville, North Carolina
252-465-4549

6. **Medical Services**
Gates County
Health Department
29 Medical Center Rd.
Gates, NC 27937
252-338-5338 or 252-357-1380

Gates County Medical Center
501 Main St.
Gatesville, NC 27938
252-357-7226

Hertford-Gates Home Health
212 Main St.
Gatesville, NC 27938
252-357-1925

7. **Medication
Assistance Program**
Gates County Department of
Social Services
122 Main St.
Gatesville, NC 27938
252-357-0075 or 252-357-1748

GoodRx
855-268-2822

NeedyMeds
800-503-6897

8. **Employment/ Vocational Rehab/ Education**
Gates Community Action
252-482-4458

Family Resource Center
794 Mid. Swamp Road
Gatesville, North Carolina
252-465-4549

NC Co-op Extension- Gates County Center
112 Court St.
Gatesville, NC 27938
252-357-1400

NC Works Career Center- Dare County
2522 S. Croatan Highway
Milepost 10.5
Nags Head, NC 27959
252-480-3500

Vocational Rehabilitation- Pasquotank County
401 S. Griffin St., Suite 100
Elizabeth City, NC 27909
252-331-4768

9. **Legal Services**
Legal Services of the Coastal Plains-Hertford County
610 E. Church St.
Ahoskie, NC 27910
252-332-5124 or 800-682-0010

10. **Recreational/ Leisure**
Gates County Community Center
130 NC Hwy158, West
Gatesville, NC 27938
252-357-0677

Merchant Meal Pond
176 Millpond Road
Gatesville, NC 27938
252-357-1191

11. **Special Populations**
Albemarle Hope Line
(Domestic Violence)
252-338-3011

Easter Seals of NC
800-662-7119

National Suicide Prevention Lifeline
800-273-TALK (8255)

Senior Citizen Center
130 NC Highway 158, East
Gatesville, NC 27938
252-357-0677

Veterans Services
112 Court St.
Gatesville, NC 27938
252-358-7811

CHAPTER 38

Graham County

1. **Mental Health and Crisis Services**
Community Connections-
Cherokee County
40 Peachtree St.
Murphy, NC 28906
828-837-0617

First at Blue Ridge-
Buncombe County
32 Knox Rd.
Ridgecrest, NC 28770
828-669-0011

2. **Substance Abuse Services**
Smoky Mountain Center, LME-
Jackson County
44 Bonnie Ln.
P.O. Box 127
Sylva, NC 28779
828-586-5501

3. **Clothing/ Food Assistance/ Financial Services**
Graham Emergency Food Bank
3734 Tallulah Rd.
Robbinsville, NC 28771
828-479-2992

WIC Program
828-479-7900

4. **Housing and Shelters**
For Square Community Action
Inc.-Cherokee County
61 Milton Mashburn Dr.
Andrews, NC 28901
828-321-4475

Independent Living-
Jackson County
122 Sylva Plaza
Sylva, North Carolina
828-586-3455

5. **Transportation**
Graham County Transportation
74 S. Main St.
Robbinsville, NC 28771
828-479-4129

6. **Medical Services**
    Graham County Health
    Department/Department of
    Public Health
    21 S. Main St.
    Robbinsville, NC 28771
    828-479-7900

7. **Medication
    Assistance Program**
    Graham County Department of
    Social Services
    191 P&J Rd.
    P.O. Box 1878
    Robbinsville, NC 28771
    828-479-7911

8. **Employment/ Vocational
    Rehab/ Education**
    NC Works Center/ ESC
    347 Rodney Orr Bypass
    Robbinsville, NC 28771
    828-479-3376

    Vocational Rehabilitation-
    Jackson County
    100 Bonnie Ln.
    Sylva, NC 28779
    828-586-1962

9. **Legal Services**
    Sylva Legal Aid-Jackson County
    1286 W. Main St.
    Sylva, North Carolina
    828-586-8931 or 800-458-6817

10. **Recreational/ Leisure**
    Fontana Dam and
    Visitors Center
    71 Fontana Rd.
    Fontana Dam, NC 28733
    828-498-2234

    Graham County Travel
    and Tourism
    387 Rodney Orr Bypass
    Robbinsville, NC 28771
    828-479-3790

11. **Special Populations**
    Graham County Senior Center
    185 W. Fort Hill Rd.
    Robbinsville, NC 28771
    828-479-7977

    Snowbird Senior Center
    157 Jackson Branch Rd.
    Robbinsville, NC 28771
    828-346-6746

    Veterans Affairs
    12 N. Main St.
    Robbinsville, NC 28771
    828-479-6653

CHAPTER 39

Granville County

1. **Mental Health and Crisis Services**
Five County MH/DD/
SA-Halifax County
210 Smith Church Road
Roanoke Rapids,
North Carolina
252-537-6174

2. **Substance Abuse Services**
VAYA Health
828-225-2785, x1512

3. **Clothing/ Food Assistance/ Financial Services**
ACIM
634 Roxboro Rd.
Oxford, NC 27565
919-690-0961

Food Pantry – Upon This Rock
1206 College St.
Oxford, NC 27565
919-692-0007

4. **Housing and Shelters**
NC Commission of
Indian Affairs
146 Main St.
Oxford, NC 27565
919-693-2456

Oxford Housing Authority
101 Hillside Dr.
Oxford, NC 27565
919-693-6936

Vance Men's Shelter
222 Young St.
Henderson, North Carolina
252-820-0701

Harbor House (Shelter)
3237 Knotts Grove Road
Oxford, NC 27565
919-690-1982

5. **Transportation**
Kerr Area Rural Travel
Transportation (KARTS)-
Vance County
1575 Ross Mill Road
Henderson, NC 27536
252-438-2573

6. **Medical Services**
Granville County
Health Department
1032 College St.
Oxford, NC 27565
919-693-2141

7. **Medication
Assistance Program**
Granville County Department
of Social Services
410 W. Spring St.
Oxford, NC 27565
919-693-1511

8. **Employment/ Vocational
Rehab/ Education**
Granville ESC
518 Lewis St.
Oxford, North Carolina
919-693-2686

NC Works Career Center-
Vance County
826 S. Garnett St.
Henderson, NC 27536
252-598-5200

Vocational Rehabilitation
402 N. Main St.
Butner, North Carolina
919-528-0227

9. **Legal Services**
Legal Aid of
NC-Durham County
201 W. Main St., Suite 400
Durham, North Carolina
919-688-6396

10. **Recreational/ Leisure**
Granville County Tourist
Information Center
124 Hillsboro St.
Oxford, NC 27565
919-693-6125

11. **Special Populations**
Families Living Violence Free
(Domestic Violence)
919-693-5700

Granville County Senior Center
107 Lanier St.
Oxford, North Carolina
919-693-1930

Granville Veteran
Services Officer
141 Williamsboro St.
Oxford, North Carolina
919-693-1484

CHAPTER 40

Greene County

1. **Mental Health and Crisis Services**
Eastpointe (Crisis Line)-800-913-6109

   Wilson-Greene Mental Health Center-Wilson County
1709 S. Tarboro St.
Wilson, North Carolina
252-399-8021

2. **Substance Abuse Services**
Friends of Philip-Narcotics Anonymous
Hookerton Recreation Park Building
484 Morris BBQ Road
Hookerton, NC 28538
800-784-9669

   Port Human Services-Pitt County
4300 Sapphire Ct., #110
Greenville, North Carolina
252-830-7540

3. **Clothing/ Food Assistance/ Financial Services**
Meals on Wheels (Seniors)
252-747-5436

   Salvation Army-Lenoir County
2110 N. Queen St.
Kinston, NC 28501
252-523-5175

4. **Housing and Shelters**
Friends of the Homeless Shelter-Lenoir County
112 N. Independence St.
Kinston, NC 28501

   Greene County Public Housing Agency
214 N. Greene Street
Snow Hill, North Carolina
252-747-8245

   SAFE-Lenoir County
Kinston, North Carolina
252-523-5573

5. *Transportation*
Greene County Transportation
104 High Main St.
Snow Hill, NC 28580
252-747-8474

6. **Medical Services**
Greene County
Health Department
227 Kingold Blvd., Suite B
Snow Hill, NC 28580
252-747-8181

Hookerton Family Practice
516 S. William Hooker Dr.
Hookerton, NC 28538

Snow Hill Medical Center
302 N. Greene St.
Snow Hill, NC 28580
252-747-2921

Walstonburg Medical Center
204 S. Main St.
Walstonburg, NC 27888
252-753-3771's

7. *Medication Assistance Program*
Greene County Department of
Social Services
227 Kingold Blvd., Suite A
Snow Hill, NC 28580
252-747-5932

8. *Employment/ Vocational Rehab/ Education*
Greene County
Education Center
818 NC Highway 91
Snow Hill, NC 28580
252-747-3434

Greene County Vocational
Rehabilitation Service-
Wilson County
306 Nash St.
Wilson, NC 27893
252-237-7161, extension 4

JobLink Career Center-
Lenoir County
Lenoir Community College
231 Highway 58, South
Kinston, NC 28502
252-527-7320

NC Cooperative Extension-
Greene County Center
229 Kingold Blvd., Suite E
Snow Hill, NC 28580
252-747-5831

NC Works Career Center
818 Highway 91, North
Snow Hill, NC 28580
252-747-5689

9. *Legal Services*
Eastern Carolina Legal
Services-Lenoir County
112 E. Blount St.
Kinston, NC 28501
252-523-5701

Legal Aid of
NC-Wilson County
208 Goldsboro St., East
Wilson, NC 27893
877-579-7562

10. *Recreational/ Leisure*

Greene County Parks
and Recreation
609 Kingold Blvd.
Snow Hill, NC 28580
252-747-2641

Greene County Visitors Center
210 N. Greene Street
Snow Hill, NC 28580
252-747-1999

11. *Special Populations*

Greene County Council
of Aging
104 Greenridge Rd.
Snow Hill, NC 28580
252-747-5436

Veterans Services
229 Kingold Blvd.
Snow Hill, North Carolina
252-747-7320

CHAPTER 41

Guilford County

1. **Mental Health and
    Crisis Services**
    Mental Health Greensboro
    (MHAG)
    700 Walter Reed Dr.
    Greensboro, NC 27403
    336-737-1402

    Monarch Behavioral Services
    201 N. Eugene St.
    Greensboro, NC 27401
    336-676-6840

    Moses Cone Behavioral
    Health Services
    510 N. Elam Ave., Suite 301
    Greensboro, NC 27403
    336-832-9800

2. **Substance Abuse Services**
    Family Service of the Piedmont
    315 E. Washington St.
    Greensboro, NC 27401
    336-387-6161 or 336-272-7273
    (Crisis Line)

Triad Behavioral Resources
810 Warren St.
Greensboro, NC 27403
336-389-1413

3. **Clothing/ Food Assistance/
    Financial Services**
    Bob's Closet (Clothes)
    1089 Knox Rd.
    McLeansville, NC 27301
    336-697-3000

    Salvation Army of Greensboro
    1311 S. Eugene St.
    Greensboro, NC 27406
    336-273-5572

4. **Housing and Shelters**
    Greensboro Housing Authority
    450 N. Church St.
    Greensboro, North Carolina
    336-275-8501

    Pathways Family Shelter
    3517 N. Church St.
    Greensboro, North Carolina
    336-271-5988

Weaver House (Shelter)
305 W. Lee St.
Greensboro, North Carolina
336-271-5985

5. **Transportation**
Access Greensboro
336-373-2634

Greensboro Transit Authority
300 W. Washington St.
Greensboro, NC 27401
336-373-2634

Piedmont Authority for
Regional Transportation
(PART)
107 Arrow Rd.
Greensboro, NC 27409
336-883-7278

6. **Medical Services**
Guilford County
Health Department
1100 E. Wendover Ave.
Greensboro, NC 27401
336-641-7777

Guilford Community
Care Network
Freeman Building
612 Pasteur Dr., Suite 108
Greensboro, NC 27406
336-895-4900

Mustard Seed
Community Health
2525-C Phillips Avenue
Greensboro, NC 27401
336-763-0814

7. **Medication
Assistance Program**
Greensboro Department of
Social Services
1203 Maple St.
Greensboro, NC 27405
336-641-3000

High Point Department of
Social Services
300 S. Centennial St.
High Point, North Carolina
336-845-7788

8. **Employment/ Vocational
Rehab/ Education**
Job Corps
230 W. Meadowview Rd.
Greensboro, NC 27407
800-733-JOBS

NC Works Career Center
230 W. Meadowview Rd.
Greensboro, NC 27407
336-297-9444

Department of
Vocational Rehabilitation
3401 W. Wendover Ave., Suite A
Greensboro, North Carolina
336-487-0500 or 336-299-7337

Department of
Vocational Rehabilitation
919 Phillips Ave., Suite 105
High Point, NC 27260
336-887-2686

9. **Legal Services**
   Legal Aid of NC
   122 N. Elm St., Suite 700
   Greensboro, NC 27401
   336-272-0148

   Women's Resource Center
   628 Summit Ave.
   Greensboro, NC 27405
   336-373-2489

10. **Recreational/Leisure**
    Visitors Center
    2411 W. Gate City Blvd.
    Greensboro, NC 27403
    800-344-2282

11. **Special Populations**
    Family Service
    (Domestic Violence)
    336-273-7273 (Greensboro)
    336-889-7273 (High Point)

    NAMI Guilford
    Crisis Line – 877-626-1772

    National Caucus & Center on
    Black Aging Inc. (NCBA)
    2301 W. Meadowview Rd.
    Greensboro, NC 27407
    336-297-9444, extension 234

    Senior Resources
    (Grandparents
    Raising Grandkids)
    1401 Benjamin Parkway
    Greensboro, NC 27408
    336-373-4816

Veteran Service Office
7325-B West Friendly
Greensboro, North Carolina
336-294-1222

Veteran Service Office
505 E. Green Dr.
High Point, North Carolina
336-845-7929

CHAPTER 42

Halifax County

1. **Mental Health and Crisis Services**
Five County MH/DD/SA
210 Smith Church Rd.
Roanoke Rapids,
North Carolina
252-537-6174

Mental Health Support
866-437-1821

2. **Substance Abuse Services**
RHA Health Services
109 W. Becker Dr.
Roanoke Rapids, NC 27870
252-537-6619

Substance Abuse Hotline
866-375-1355

3. **Clothing/ Food Assistance/ Financial Services**
Hannah's Closet
1034 Roanoke Ave.
Roanoke Rapids, NC 27870
252-541-1127

Union Mission of Roanoke
Rapids (Food/Clothing)
1310 Roanoke Ave.
Roanoke Rapids, NC 27870
252-537-3372

4. **Housing and Shelters**
Ahoskie Housing Authority-
Hertford County
200 Pierce Ave.
Ahoskie, NC 27910
252-537-0552

Roanoke Rapids
Housing Authority
200 Creekside Ct.
Roanoke Rapids,
North Carolina
252-537-0552

Roanoke Rapids
Housing Authority
949 Roanoke Ave.
Roanoke Rapids, NC 27870
252-308-0693

Union Mission of Roanoke
Rapids (Shelter)
1310 Roanoke Ave.
Roanoke Rapids, NC 27870
252-537-3370

5. **Transportation**
Choanoke Public
Transportation Authority-
Northampton County
505 N. Main St.
Rich Square, NC 27869
252-539-2022

6. **Medical Services**
Halifax County
Health Department
19 N. Dobbs St.
Halifax, NC 27839
252-583-5021 or 252-534-5841

7. **Medication
Assistance Program**
Halifax County Department of
Social Services
4421 Highway 301
Halifax, NC 27839
252-536-2511

8. **Employment/ Vocational
Rehab/ Education**
NC Works Career Center
1560 Julian R.
Alllsbrook Highway
Roanoke Rapids, NC 27870
252-507-6180

Vocational Rehabilitation
615 Julian Alsbrook Highway
Roanoke Rapids,
North Carolina
252-537-1126

9. **Legal Services**
Legal Aid of NC-
Hertford County
610 E. Church St.
Ahoskie, North Carolina
252-332-5124

10. **Recreational/ Leisure**
Halifax County Visitor Center
260 Premier Blvd.
Roanoke Rapids, NC 27870
252-535-1687

11. **Special Populations**
Halifax County Veteran
Services Office
26 N. King St.
Halifax, NC 27839
282-583-1688

Jo Story Senior Center
701 Jackson St.
Roanoke Rapids, NC 27870
252-533-2847

CHAPTER 43

Harnett County

1. **Mental Health and Crisis Services**
Moore County Sandhills Center
for MH/DD/SA
P.O. Box 9
West End, NC 27367
910-673-9111

2. **Substance Abuse Services**
DayMark Recovery Services
5841 US Highway 421 S.
Lillington, NC 27506
910-893-5727 or 866-275-9552

3. **Clothing/ Food Assistance/ Financial Services**
Salvation Army of
Harnett County
406 W. Cumberland St.
Dunn, NC 28334
910-892-2902

Harnett Food Pantry
413 W. Old Rd.
Lillington, NC 27546
910-985-7787

4. **Housing and Shelters**
Beacon Rescue Mission
of Dunn
207 W. Broad Street
Dunn, North Carolina
910-892-5772

Dunn Housing Authority
601 E. Canary St.
Dunn, NC 28334
910-819-5076

Harnett County
Housing Authority
103 E. Ivey Street
Lillington, NC 27546
910-893-7560

5. **Transportation**
Harnett Area Rural Transit
System (HARTS)
910-814-4019

6. **Medical Services**
Harnett County
Health Department
307 Cornelius Harnett Blvd.
Lillington, North Carolina
910-893-7550

Tri-County
Community Healthcare
3331 Easy St.
Dunn, NC 28334
910-567-6194

7. **Medication Assistance Program**
Harnett County Department of
Social Services
311 W. Cornelius Harnett Blvd.
Lillington, NC 27546
910-893-7500

8. **Employment/ Vocational Rehab/ Education**
JobsLink
1137 E. Cornelius Harnett Blvd.
Lillington, NC 27546
910-814-4042

Vocational Rehabilitation
214 W. Edgerton
Dunn, North Carolina
910-892-7040

9. **Legal Services**
Legal Aid of North Carolina
327 Dick St.
Fayetteville, North Carolina
910-483-0400

10. **Recreational/ Leisure**
Harnett County Visitor Center
103 E. Cumberland St.
Dunn, NC 28334
910-892-3282

11. **Special Populations**
Coats Senior Center
603 E. Stewart St.
Coats, NC 27541
910-897-4616

Dunn Senior
Enrichment Center
640 E. Johnson St.
Dunn, NC 28334
910-814-8929

Harnett County
Veteran Services
420 McKinney Pkwy.
Lillington, NC 27546
910-893-7555

Harnett County Veterans
Services Officer
303 W. Duncan St.
Lillington, North Carolina
910-893-7574

CHAPTER 44

Haywood County

1. **Mental Health and Crisis Services**
Meridian Behavioral Health
Services-Blue Ridge Health
490 Hospital Dr.
Clyde, NC 28721
828-246-6372

2. **Substance Abuse Services**
Appalachian Community
Services-Smokey Mountain
Center-Jackson County
P.O. Box 127
Sylva, North Carolina
828-586-5501

3. **Clothing/ Food Assistance/ Financial Services**
Haywood Pathways Center
179 Hemlock St.
Waynesville, NC 28786
828-246-0332

Salvation Army
Mountain Mission
290 Pigeon St.
Waynesville, NC 28786
828-456-7111

Community Kitchen
828-648-0014

4. **Housing and Shelters**
Pathways
179 Hemlock St.
Waynesville, NC 28786
828-452-3846 or 828-246-0332

Waynesville Housing Authority
48 Chestnut Park Dr.
Waynesville, NC 28786
828-456-3377

5. **Transportation**
Haywood Public Transit
50 Armory Dr.
Clyde, NC 28721
828-565-0362

Mountain Projects
828-452-1447

6. **Medical Services**
Haywood Health Department
828-454-5287

Midway Medical Center
6750 Carolina Blvd.
Clyde, NC 28721
828-627-2211

7. **Medication
Assistance Program**
Haywood County Department
of Social Services
486 E. Marshall Street
Waynesville, NC 28786
828-452-6620

Health and Human Services
157 Paragon Pkwy.
Clyde, NC 28721
828-452-6620

8. **Employment/ Vocational
Rehab/ Education**
NC Works/Employment
Security Commission
1170 N. Main St.
Waynesville, NC 28786
828-456-6061

9. **Legal Services**
Pisgah Legal Aid-
Buncombe County
P.O. Box 2276
Asheville, NC 28802
866-253-0406 or 800-489-6144

Sylva Legal Aid-Jackson County
1286 W. Main St.
Sylva, North Carolina
800-458-6817

Legal Aid of North Carolina
800-458-6817

Magistrate Office
828-456-8191

10. **Recreational/ Leisure**
Haywood County
Visitors Center
1110 Soco Rd.
Maggie Valley, NC 28751
828-944-0761

11. **Special Populations**
Haywood County Senior
Resource Center
81 Elmwood Way
Waynesville, NC 28786
828-356-2800

Veteran Services
828-452-6634

CHAPTER 45

Henderson County

1. **Mental Health and Crisis Services**
Little Gerald Services
120 Chadwick Ave., Suite 3
Hendersonville, NC 28792

   Pardee Hospital-Mental
Health Clinic
800 N. Justice St.
Hendersonville, NC 28791
828-696-1000

2. **Substance Abuse Services**
Advent Health
100 Hospital Dr.
Hendersonville, NC
828-684-8501

   Pieridae Treatment Centers
4806 Asheville Hwy.
Hendersonville, NC 28791
828-595-9300

3. **Clothing/ Food Assistance/ Financial Services**
The Salvation Army
239 3rd Ave., East
Hendersonville, NC 28792
828-693-4181

   The Storehouse
1049 Spartanburg Hwy.
Hendersonville, NC 28792
828-692-8300

4. **Housing and Shelters**
Hendersonville
Housing Authority
203 N. Justice St.
Hendersonville, North
Carolina 28793
828-692-6175

   Henderson Rescue Mission
Hendersonville, North Carolina
828-697-1354

Housing
Assistance Corporation
602 Kanuga Rd.
Hendersonville, NC
828-692-4744

5. *Transportation*
Apple Country Transit
220 King Creek Blvd.
Hendersonville, NC 28793
828-693-1711

WNC Source
Community Transportation
526 7th Ave., East
Hendersonville, NC 28792
828-698-8571

6. *Medical Services*
Department of Public Health
1200 Spartanburg Hwy.,
Suite 100
Hendersonville, NC 28792
828-692-4223

Free Clinics
841 Case St.
Hendersonville, North Carolina
828-697-8422

7. *Medication
Assistance Program*
Henderson County Department
of Social Services
1200 Spartanburg Hwy.,
Suite 300
Hendersonville, NC 28792
828-697-5500

8. *Employment/ Vocational
Rehab/ Education*
NC Vocational Rehabilitation
578 Upward Road, Unit 6
Flat Rock, NC 28731
828-692-9184

9. *Legal Services*
Pisgah Legal Services
440 S. Church Street
Hendersonville, NC 28792
828-253-0406 or 800-489-6144

10. *Recreational/ Leisure*
Hendersonville Visitor Center
201 S. Main St.
Hendersonville, NC 28792
828-693-9708

11. *Special Populations*
Council on Aging
105 King Creek Blvd.
Hendersonville, NC 28792
828-692-4203

National Suicide Line
988

SAFELIGHT
(Domestic Violence)
828-693-3840

Veteran's Crisis Line
800-273-8255, press 1

Veteran Services
828-697-4817

CHAPTER 46

Hertford County

1. **Mental Health and Crisis Services**
   Integrated Family Services
   312 Academy St., Suite B
   Ahoskie, NC 27910
   252-209-03884 Crisis Line
   866-437-1821

   Northside Behavioral Health
   111 Hertford County High Rd.
   Ahoskie, NC 27910
   252-209-3056

   Trillium Health Resources
   144 Community College Rd.
   Ahoskie, NC 27910
   866-998-9725 or Crisis Services
   877-685-2415

   Vidant Behavioral Health
   113-B Hertford County
   High Road
   Ahoskie, NC 27910

2. **Substance Abuse Services**
   NC Quit Line
   (Smoking Cessation)
   800-784-8669

   PORT Health Services
   1311 1st St., West
   Ahoskie, NC 27910
   252-332-5036

3. **Clothing/ Food Assistance/ Financial Services**
   Ahoskie Food Pantry
   701 E. Church St.
   Ahoskie, NC 27910
   252-209-0540

   Choanoke Area
   Development Association-
   Community Action Program
   105 N. Academy St., Building B
   Ahoskie, NC 27910
   252-398-4131

Food Bank of the Albemarle
200 W. Main St.
Murfreesboro, NC 27855
252-209-0540

WIC Clinic
252-862-4217

4. *Housing and Shelters*
Ahoskie Housing Authority
200 Pierce Ave.
Ahoskie, NC 27910
252-332-4104

CADA
105 N. Academy St.
Ahoskie, NC 27910
252-332-2692

Catholic Charities
252-426-7717

Domestic Violence Shelter
Ahoskie, North Carolina
252-332-1933

Forest Meadows
Housing Authority
103 Land Ct.
Winton, North Carolina
919-537-1051

SAFE (Domestic Violence
Emergency Shelter)
P.O. Box 444
Winton, NC 27986
252-332-4047

5. *Transportation*
Choanoke Public
Transportation Authority
(CPTA)-Northampton County
505 N. Main St.
Rich Square, NC 27869
252-539-2022

Medex Medical Transport
902 E. Memorial Dr.
Ahoskie, NC 27190
252-332-4555

6. *Medical Services*
Hertford County Public
Health Department
801 N. King St.
Winton, NC 27986
252-358-7833

Hertford County Public
Health Department
828 S. Academy St.
Ahoskie, NC 27910
252-862-4054

Roanoke Chowan Community
Health Center
120 Health Center Dr.
Ahoskie, NC 27910
252-209-0237

Vidant Roanoke-
Chowan Hospital
500 S. Academy Street
Ahoskie, NC 27910
252-209-3000

7. *Medication Assistance Program*
GoodyRx
855-268-2822

Hertford County Department
of Social Services
704 N. King St.
Winton, North Carolina
252-358-7830

NeedyMeds
800-503-6897

8. *Employment/ Vocational Rehab/ Education*
Hertford County Job Link
Center/ESC
1114 N. Academy St.
Ahoskie, NC 27910
252-332-5016

NC Works
109 Community College Rd.
Ahoskie, NC 27910
252-862-1257

9. *Legal Services*
Legal Aid of NC
610 E. Church St.
Ahoskie, NC 27910
252-332-5124

10. *Recreational/ Leisure*
Ahoskie Parks
252-332-5146

Ahoskie Recreational Complex
1103 W. Main St.
Ahoskie, NC 27910

Gallery Theatre
115 W. Main St.
Ahoskie, NC 27910
252-332-2976

Parks and
Recreation Commission
115 Justice Dr., Suite 1
Winton, NC 27986
252-358-7805

Winton River Park
King Street
Winton, NC 27986

11. *Special Populations*
Domestic Violence Support
Group- SAFE
Ahoskie, North Carolina
252-332-1933

Family Resource Center
of Ahoskie
217 W. Church St.
Ahoskie, NC 27910
252-862-4777

Hertford County Senior Center
408 S. Camp St.
Winton, North Carolina
252-358-7856

Senior Center (Nutrition)
320 W. Main St.
Murfreesboro, NC 27855
252-358-7856

Veterans Services
704 N. King St.
Winton, NC 27986
252-358-7811

CHAPTER 47

Hoke County

1. *Mental Health and Crisis Services*
Health Care Connections
402 S. Main St.
Raeford, North Carolina
910-904-6600

Sandhills Center, LME
121 E. Elwood Ave.
Raeford, NC 28376
910-875-8156

2. *Substance Abuse Services*
DayMark Recovery Services
121 E. Elwood Ave.
Raeford, NC 28376
910-875-8156

Primary Health Choice
512 Harris Ave.
Raeford, NC 28376
910-875-1485

3. *Clothing/ Food Assistance/ Financial Services*
Hoke Emergency Liaison
Program (HELP)
110 E. Central Ave.
Raeford, NC 28376
910-875-8857

Word of Life Temple, Inc.
1988 Fayetteville Rd.
Raeford, NC 28376
910-875-6990

WIC Clinic
910-875-2298

4. *Housing and Shelters*
Catholic Charities
910-424-2020

Four-County Community
Services-Scotland County
241 S. Main St., Suite 200
Laurinburg, NC 28352
910-291-3054

Southeastern Community and Family Services, Inc.
910-875-5536

5. *Transportation*
Hoke Area Transit System
316 S. Magnolia St.
Raeford, NC 28376
910-875-8696

Waccamaw Transport
150 Paint Rd.
Raeford, NC 28376
919-965-6311, extension 5

6. *Medical Services*
Cape Fear Valley
Medical Center
405 S. Main St.
Raeford, NC 28376
910-615-5800

Hoke County
Health Department
689 E. Palmer Rd.
Raeford, NC 28376
910-875-3717

**7. *Medication
Assistance Program***
Hoke County Department of
Social Services
314 S. Magnolia St.
Raeford, NC 28376
910-875-8725

NeedyMeds
800-503-6897

**8. *Employment/ Vocational
Rehab/ Education***
ESC/ Job Link Center
310 Birch St.
Raeford, NC 28376
910-875-5059

Maggie's Outreach Community
Economic Development Center
7350 Turnpike Road
Raeford, NC 28376
910-875-6623

Vocational Rehabilitation
150 Lake Blvd.
Pinehurst, NC 28347
910-295-1530

9. *Legal Services*
Legal Aid
910-521-2831

Legal Aid of
NC-Cumberland County
3827 Dick St., Suite 103
Fayetteville, NC 28301
910-438-0400

10. *Recreational/ Leisure*
Hoke County Co-op Ext.
116 W. Prospect Ave., Stop1
Raeford, NC 28376
910-875-3461

Raeford-Hoke Museum
111 S. Highland St.
Raeford, NC 28376
910-875-2279

11. Special Populations

Hoke County Senior Center
423 E. Central Ave.
Raeford, NC 28376
910-875-8588

Veteran Services
129 W. Elwood St.
Raeford, NC 28347
910-875-2147

CHAPTER 48

Hyde County

1. **Mental Health and Crisis Services**
ECU Health Behavioral Health
305 Back Rd.
Ocracoke, NC 27960
252-928-6580

Vidant Behavioral Health
1221 Main St.
Swan Quarter, NC 27885
252-926-3751

2. **Substance Abuse Services**
Alcoholics Anonymous
252-975-6113
Hotline – 800-350-2538

NC Quit Line
(Smoking Cessation)
800-784-8669

Ocracoke Medical Center
305 Back Rd.
Ocracoke, NC 27960
252-928-1511

Substance Abuse and Mental
Health Services Administration
(SAMHSA)
800-662-4357

3. **Clothing/ Food Assistance/ Financial Services**
Food Pantry
4240 Highway 264
Scranton, NC 27875
252-394-6461

Hyde County Hotline
Thrift Store
34818 US Highway 264
Engelhard, NC 27824
252-925-1031

Village Thrift
271 Irvin Garrish Hwy.
Ocracoke, NC 27960
252-928-2855

WIC Clinic
252-926-4399

4. **Housing and Shelters**

Mid-East Regional Housing
Authority-Martin County
415 East Blvd., Suite 140
Williamston, NC 27892
252-789-4926

NWBD
30 Oyster Creek Rd.
Swan Quarter, NC 27885
252-312-6859

5. **Transportation**

Hyde Transit Services
1275 Main St.
Swan Quarter, NC 27885
252-926-2163

Swan Quarter Ferry
748 Oyster Creek Rd.
Swan Quarter, North Carolina
252-791-3300

6. **Medical Services**

Cross Creek Healthcare
1719 Quarter Rd.
Swan Quarter, North Carolina
252-928-1511

Engelhard Medical Center
33270 US Highway 264
Engelhard, NC 27824
252-925-7000

Hyde County
Health Department
1151 Main St.
Swan Quarter, NC 27885
252-926-4200

7. **Medication
Assistance Program**

GoodRx
855-268-2822

Hyde County Department of
Social Services
35015 US Highway 264
Engelhard, NC 27824
252-926-4476

NeedyMeds
800-503-6897

8. **Employment/ Vocational
Rehab/ Education**

Hyde County JobLink
1430 Main St.
Swan Quarter, NC 27885
252-926-9272

Job Corps
800-773-5627

9. **Legal Services**

Legal Aid of NC-
Hertford County
610 E. Church St.
Ahoskie, NC 27910
252-332-5124

Legal Aid of NC- Pitt County
301 Evans St., Suite 102
Greenville, NC 27858
252-758-0113

10. Recreational/Leisure

Davis Youth Recreation and
Community Center
33472 US Highway 274
Engelhard, NC 27824
252-925-3970

Hyde County Recreation
252-926-3715

Mattamuskeet National
Wildlife Refuge
Mattamuskeet Road
Swan Quarter, NC 27885
252-926-4021

Mattie Arts and Visitors Center
35 NC Highway 45
Swan Quarter, NC 27885
252-926-2787

Ocracoke Lighthouse
Lighthouse Road
Ocracoke, NC 27960

11. Special Populations

Hyde County Hotline
(Domestic Violence)
252-925-2500

Hyde County Mattamuskeet
Senior Center
160 Juniper Bay Road
Swan Quarter, NC 27885
252-926-1956

Veterans Services Office
23145 US Highway 264
Swan Quarter, NC 27885
252-926-5280

CHAPTER 49

Iredell County

1. **Mental Health and Crisis Services**
   CareNet Counseling
   146 E. McClelland Ave.
   Mooresville, NC 28115
   704-665-0352

   Dove House
   2407 Simonton Rd.
   Statesville, NC 28625
   704-883-9814

   National Alliance of Mental
   Illness (NAMI)
   Helpline – 800-950-6264

2. **Substance Abuse Services**
   Addiction Recovery Medical
   Service (ARMS)
   536 Signal Hill Dr.
   Statesville, NC 28625
   704-872-0234

   DayMark Recovery
   518 Signal Hill Dr., Ext.
   Statesville, NC 28625
   704-873-1114

3. **Clothing/ Food Assistance/ Financial Services**
   Community Kitchen
   1421 5th St.
   Statesville, NC 28687
   704-872-4045

   Feed NC
   275 S. Broad Street
   Mooresville, NC 28115
   704-660-9010

   Salvation Army
   1361 Caldwell Street
   Statesville North
   Carolina 28677
   704-872-5623

   WIC of Iredell County
   704-878-5319

4. **Housing and Shelters**
   5th St. Shelter
   1400 5th St.
   Statesville, North Carolina
   704-872-4045

Mooresville Housing
1046 N. Main St.
Mooresville, North Carolina
704-664-1659

Statesville Housing
110 W. Allison St.
Statesville, North Carolina
704-872-9811

5. **Transportation**
ICATS
261 Ebony Cir.
Statesville, NC 28627
704-873-9393

6. **Medical Services**
Mooresville Health Department
610 E. Center Ave.
Mooresville, NC 28115
704-664-5281

7. **Medication Assistance Program**
GoodRx
855-268-2822

Iredell County Department of
Social Services
549 Eastside Dr.
Statesville, NC 28625
704-873-5631

NeedyMeds
800-503-6897

8. **Employment/ Vocational Rehab/ Education**
NC Works Career Center
133 Island Ford Rd.
Statesville, NC 28625
704-878-4241

Employment Security
Commission (ESC)
888-737-0259

9. **Legal Services**
Legal Aid-Forsyth County
102 W. 3rd St., #460
Winston-Salem, NC 27101
336-725-9162 or 866-219-5262

10. **Recreational/ Leisure**
Statesville Convention and
Visitors Bureau
328 E. Broad Street
Statesville, NC 28677
704-878-3480

Visitor Center
759 State Park Rd.
Troutman, NC 28166

11. **Special Populations**
Elder Center
502 Brevard St.
Statesville, NC 28677
704-873-0702

Immediate Food Aid Hotline
866-348-6479

Iredell Info & Referral
1835 Daily Ave.
Statesville, North Carolina
704-872-2900

Safe Alliance
(Domestic Violence)
704-665-8745

Senior Center
344 E. Front St.
Statesville, NC 28677
704-873-5171

Veterans Services
610 E. Center Ave.
Mooresville, NC 28115
704-664-3869

CHAPTER 50

Jackson County

1. **Mental Health and Crisis Services**
Meridian Behavioral
44 Bonnie Ln.
Sylva, NC 28779
828-631-3973

Smokey Mountain Center for MH, SA, & IDD
828-586-5501

Sylva Clinical
70 Westcare Drive, Suite 402
Sylva, NC 28779
828-586-5555

2. **Substance Abuse Services**
Meridian Behavioral
44 Bonnie Ln.
Sylva, NC 28779
828-631-3973

3. **Clothing/ Food Assistance/ Financial Services**
Fishes and Loaves
549 Frank Allen Rd.
Cashiers, NC 28717
828-508-0378

The Community Table of Sylva
23 Central St.
Sylva, NC 28779
828-586-6782

WIC Clinic
828- 587-8243

4. **Housing and Shelters**
Jackson County
Housing Authority
401 Grindstaff Cove Rd.
Sylva, North Carolina
828-631-2292

Mountain Projects
154 Medical Park Loop
Sylva, NC 28779
828-586-2345

5. **Transportation**
Jackson County Transit
1148 Haywood Rd.
Sylva, NC 28779
828-586-0233

6. **Medical Services**
Jackson County Department of
Public Health
538 Scott Creek Rd.
Sylva, NC 28779
828-586-8994

7. **Medication
Assistance Program**
Jackson County Department of
Social Services
15 Griffin St.
Sylva, NC 28779
828-586-5546

8. **Employment/ Vocational
Rehab/ Education**
NC Works Career Center
26 Ridgeway Street
Sylva, NC 28779
828-586-4063

Vocational Rehabilitation
100 Bonnie Ln., Suite A
Sylva, NC 28779
828-313-5100 or 877-282-0753

9. **Legal Services**
Sylva Legal Aid
1286 W. Main St.
Sylva, North Carolina
828-586-8931 or 800-458-6817

10. **Recreational/ Leisure**
Jackson County Visitors Center
773 W. Main St.
Sylva, NC 28779
828-586-2155

11. **Special Populations**
BREACH of Jackson County
(Domestic Violence)
1414 E. Main St.
Sylva, North Carolina
828-631-4488

Jackson County Veterans Office
111 Central St.
Sylva, NC 28779
828-586-7508

Senior Center/Department
on Aging
100 County Services Park
Sylva, NC 28779
828-586-5494

CHAPTER 51

Johnston County

1. **Mental Health and Crisis Services**
A New Start Support Services
540 W. Main St., #100
Clayton, NC 27530
919-359-0669

Johnson County Mental
Health/Substance Abuse Center
521 N. Brightleaf Blvd.
Smithfield, NC 27577
919-989-5500

Therapeutic Alternatives-
Mobile Crisis
26 Noble St.
Smithfield, NC 27577
877-626-1772

2. **Substance Abuse Services**
AA
800-372-5447

Family Counseling House
of Hope
408 Covered Bridge Road
Clayton, NC 27520
919-550-8181

First Baptist Church
202 S. 4th St.
Smithfield, NC 27577
919-934-9771

Johnson County Mental
Health/Substance
Abuse Program
910-989-5500

3. **Clothing/ Food Assistance/ Financial Services**
A Touch From Above Faith
Center (Food)
654 Main St.
Wilson's Mills, North Carolina
919-938-0073

Area Christians Together
in Service (ACTS)-
(Clothes Closet)
1204 N. Johnson St.
Benson, NC 27504
919-820-1591

Building 323 (Food)
73 Wilder Rd.
Middlesex, North Carolina
919-269-9207

Changing Heart Deliverance
House of Praise (Food)
102 Holts Pond Rd.
Princeton, North Carolina
919-502-2746

First Baptist Church
403 N. Main St.
Four Oaks, NC 27524
919-963-2102

Good News Buenas
Nuevas Ministry
2176-D US 70 Hwy Alt
Pine Level, North Carolina
919-617-2108

Kenly Area Ministries (Food)
212 W. 2nd St.
Kenly, North Carolina
919-284-2449

St. Ann's Catholic Church
(Utilities Assistance)
4057 US 70 W., Business
Clayton, NC 27530
919-934-9546

Salvation Army
306 N. Brightleaf Blvd.
Smithfield, NC 27577
919-934-9102

Shiloh Christian Church
(Soup Kitchen)
209 Durham St.
Smithfield, NC 27577
919-934-0278

WIC Clinic
919-989-5255

4. *Housing and Shelters*
Benson Housing Authority
413 Williams Dr.
Benson, NC 27504
919-894-8216, x 24

Catholic Charities
919-947-0807

Day by Day (Shelter)
312 S. Webb St.
Selma, NC 27576
919-965-6550 or 919-965-9927

Faith Mission
931 Blount St.
Smithfield, NC 27577
919-934-3765

Good Neighbor House
(Women)
523 Glenn St.
Smithfield, NC 27577
919-934-3639

Johnston County
Halfway House
407 W. Watson
Selma, NC 27576
919-965-6333

Selma Housing Authority
711 E. Lizzie St.
Selma, NC 27576
919-965-3755

Smithfield Housing Authority
801 S. 5th St.
Smithfield, NC 27577
919-934-9491

Smithfield Rescue Mission
(Men)
523 Glenn St.
Smithfield, NC 27577
919-934-9257

5. *Transportation*
Johnston County Area
Transportation Service (JCATS)
1050 W. Noble St.
Selma, NC 27576
919-202-5030

6. *Medical Services*
Johnston County
Health Department
517 N. Brightleaf Blvd.
Smithfield, NC 27557
919-989-5200

7. *Medication*
Assistance Program
GoodRx
855-268-2822

Johnston County Department
of Social Services
714 North St.
Smithfield, NC 27577
919-989-5300

NeedyMeds
800-503-6897

8. *Employment/ Vocational*
Rehab/ Education
Cooperative Extension Service
2736 Highway 210
Smithfield, NC 27597
919-553-0953

JobLink Career Center
300 S. 3rd St., Suite A
Smithfield, NC 27577
919-209-2094

Johnston County
Industries, Inc.
1100 E. Preston St.
Selma, NC 27576
919-743-8700, extension 247

NC Works Career Center
8998 US Highway 70
W., Business
Suite 100
Clayton, NC 27520
919-553-0953

Vocational Rehabilitation
18 Noble St.
Smithfield, NC 27557
919-934-0525

9. *Legal Services*
East Community Legal Services
212 Church St.
Selma, North Carolina
919-934-5027

Legal Aid of NC Inc.
300 S. 3rd St., Suite A
Smithfield, NC 27577
919-934-5027 or 866-219-5262

10. *Recreational/ Leisure*
Johnston County
Visitors Bureau
234 Ventura Dr.
Smithfield, NC 27577
919-989-8687

The Boys and Girls Club
609 N. Pollocks St.
Selma, NC 27576
919-965-5240

11. *Special Populations*
Clayton Senior Center
303 Dairy Rd.
Clayton, NC 27520
919-553-4350

Community and Senior Service
1363 W. Market St.
Smithfield, NC 27577
919-934-6042

Harbor Inc.
(Domestic Violence)
919-934-0233

Johnston County
Veterans Officer
212 E. Market Street, Room 303
Smithfield, NC 27577
919-989-5067

CHAPTER 52

Jones County

1. **Mental Health and Crisis Services**
Neuse Mental Health Center
1311 Health Dr.
New Bern, North Carolina
252-636-1510

RHA Health Service
104 Pirates Rd.
New Bern, NC 28562
919-803-2963 or 800-848-0180
Crisis Line – 844-709-4097

2. **Substance Abuse Services**
Coastal Coalition for Substance
Abuse Program (CCSAP)
601 Broad Street
New Bern, NC 28563
252-649-1615

Trillium Health Resources-
Pitt County
201 W. 1st St.
Greenville, NC 27858
866-998-2597 or 877-685-2415

3. **Clothing/ Food Assistance/ Financial Services**
Jones County Community
of Hope
433 1st St.
Trenton, NC 28585
252-670-7093

Jones County R.I.S.E.
(Emergency Assistance)
389 NC Highway 58 S.
Trenton, North Carolina
252-397-0336

SNAP Program
252-448-2581

The Filling Station-Food Pantry
221 Main St.
Pollocksvillle, NC 28573
252-224-1127

Trenton Food Pantry
252-723-0049

Trenton Methodist Church-
Food Pantry
107 Market St.
Trenton, North Carolina
252-448-1133

WIC Clinic
252-448-9111

4. **Housing and Shelters**
Catholic Charities
252-638-2188

Coastal Community Action
303 McQueen Avenue
Newport, NC 28570
252-223-1630

Coastal Women's Shelter
134 Industrial Park Dr.
Trenton, NC 28585
252-448-9971 or (Crises Line)
252-638-5995

5. **Transportation**
Craven Area Rural
Transit System (CARTS)-
Craven County
1106 Clarks Rd.
New Bern, NC 28562
252-636-4917 or 800-735-2962

6. **Medical Services**
Jones County
Health Department
418 NC Highway 58 N., Unit C
Trenton, NC 28585
252-448-9111

MERCI Clinic
1315 Tatum Dr.
New Bern, NC 28560
252-633-1599

7. **Medication
Assistance Program**
Jones County Department of
Social Services
418 NC Highway 58 N., Unit D
Trenton, NC 28585
252-448-2581

8. **Employment/ Vocational
Rehab/ Education**
NC Division of Vocational
Rehabilitation-Craven County
2832 Neuse Boulevard
New Bern, NC 28562
252-514-4727 or 877-858-8470

NC Works Career Center
509 NC Highway 58 N.
Trenton, NC 28585
252-448-5021, extension 790

9. **Legal Services**
Legal Aid of NC- Pitt County
301 Evans St., Suite 102
Greenville, NC 27858
252-758-0113 or 800-682-4592

10. **Recreational/ Leisure**
Jones County Parks
and Recreation
418 Highway 58 N.
Trenton, NC 28585
919-675-4145

11. *Special Populations*

HOPE4NC (Mental Health)
Crisis Line – 855-587-3463

Jones County Senior Center
147 Franck's Field Rd.
Trenton, NC 28585
252-448-1001

Jones County Veteran
Services Office
145 Francks Field Road
Trenton, NC 28585
252-448-1121

NC211 (Referral Service)
888-892-1162 or 211
Veterans Crisis Line
800-273-8255

CHAPTER 53

Lee County

1. **Mental Health and Crisis Services**
Meaningful Mind Counseling
607 Weaver St.
Sanford, NC 27330
919-292-2614

   Sandy Hills Center for MH/
DD/SA-Moore County
P.O. Box 9
West End, NC 27367
910-673-9111 or 800-256-2452

2. **Substance Abuse Services**
DayMark Recovery Services
130 Carbonton Road
Sanford, NC 27330
919-774-6521

   Sanford Treatment Center
280 Industrial Dr.
Sanford, NC 27330
919-776-0711

3. **Clothing/ Food Assistance/ Financial Services**
Bread of Life
219 Maple Ave.
Sanford, NC 27330
919-777-7233

   Breadbasket of Samford
140 E. Chisholm St.
Sanford, NC 27330
919-774-3118

   Salvation Army (Clothes)
507 N. Steele St.
Sanford, NC 27330
919-718-1717

4. **Housing and Shelters**
Haven (Shelter)
215 Bracken St.
Sanford, NC 27330
919-774-8923

   Sanford Housing Authority
1000 Carthage St.
Sanford, NC 27330
919-776-7655

5. ***Transportation***
County of Lee Transit
System-C.O.L.T.S.
1615 S. 3rd St.
Sanford, NC 27330
919-776-7201

6. ***Medical Services***
Helping Hands Clinic
507 N. Steele St.
Sanford, NC 27330
919-776-4359

Lee County Health Department
106 Hillcrest Dr.
Sanford, North Carolina
919-718-4640

7. ***Medication
Assistance Program***
GoodRx
855-268-2822

Lee County Department of
Social Services
530 Carthage St.
Sanford, NC 27330
919-718-4690

NeedyMeds
800-503-6897

8. ***Employment/ Vocational
Rehab/ Education***
NC Works Career Center
1909 Lee Ave.
Sanford, NC 27330
919-775-2241

Vocational Rehabilitation
112 Dennis Dr.
Sanford, NC 27330
919-579-5120

Vocational Rehabilitation
201 Commercial Ct.
Sanford, North Carolina
919-775-2247

9. ***Legal Services***
Legal Aid of NC
503 Carthage St., Suite 305
Sanford, North Carolina
919-774-6241

10. ***Recreational/ Leisure***
Sanford Welcome Center
229 Carthage St.
Sanford, NC 27330
919-718-4659

11. ***Special Populations***
Lee Veteran Services Officer
106 Hillcrest Dr.
Sanford, North Carolina
919-718-4620

Senior Services
1605 S. 3rd St.
Sanford, NC 27330
919-776-0501

CHAPTER 54

Lenoir County

1. **Mental Health and Crisis Services**
Eastpointe Human Services-
Edgecombe County
500 Nash Med. Arts Mall
Rocky Mount, North Carolina
252-937-8141 or 800-913-6109

Lenoir County Mental Health
2901 N. Heritage St.
Kinston, NC 28501
252-527-7086

2. **Substance Abuse Services**
AA Information Line
800-372-5447

PORT Human Services
2901 N. Heritage St.
Kinston, NC 28501
252-233-2383

3. **Clothing/ Food Assistance/ Financial Services**
Goodwill
4190 W. Vernon Ave.
Kinston, NC 28504
252-520-6624

Home Delivered Meals
252-527-9561 or 800-926-4442

Mary's Kitchen
110 N. Independence St.
Kinston, NC 28501
252-523-1013

Salvation Army
2110 N. Queen St.
Kinston, NC 28501
252-523-5175

4. **Housing and Shelters**
Flynn Christian Fellowship
Home (Men)
611 Mitchell St.
Kinston, North Carolina
252-523-6621

Friends of the Homeless Shelter
112 N. Independence St.
Kinston, NC 28501
252-522-2788 or 252-933-6662

Kinston Housing Authority
697 N. Queen St.
Kinston, NC 28501
252-52 3-1195

5. *Transportation*
Lenoir County Transit
201 E. King St.
Kinston, NC 28501
252-559-6457

6. *Medical Services*
Interim Healthcare
(Home Health)
400 Glenwood Ave.
Kinston, NC 28501
252-526-9792

Kinston Community
Health Center
324 N. Queen St.
Kinston, NC 28501
252-522-9800

Lenoir County
Health Department
201 N. McLewean Street
Kinston, NC 28501
252-526-4200

Lenoir Memorial Hospital
100 Airport Rd.
Kinston, NC 28501
252-522-7171

7. *Medication
Assistance Program*
Lenoir County Department of
Social Services
130 W. King St.
Kinston, NC 28501
252-523-1013

GoodRx
855-268-2822

NeedyMeds
800-503-6897

8. *Employment/ Vocational
Rehab/ Education*
Job Link Career Center
Lenoir Community College
231 Highway 58, South
Kinston, NC 28502
252-527-7320

NC Works Center
231 Highway 58, South
Kinston, NC 28501
252-775-6021

9. *Legal Services*
East Carolina Legal Services
112 E. Blount St.
Kinston, NC 28501
252-523-5701

10. *Recreational/ Leisure*
Kinston/Lenoir Parks and
Recreation Department
2602 W. Vernon St.
Kinston, NC 28501
252-939-3332

Young Women's
Outreach Center
119 E. Blount St.
Kinston, NC 28501
252-527-7844

11. *Special Populations*
Lenoir County Council
on Aging
112 E. Blount St.
Kinston, NC 28502
252-527-1545

National Call Center for
Homeless Veterans
877-424-3838

SAFE (Domestic Violence-
women and kids)
208 Glenwood Ave.
Kinston, NC 28504
252-523-5573

Veteran's Affairs
1136 US Highway 258, North
Suite 101
Kinston, NC 28504
252-522-5050

CHAPTER 55

Lincoln County

1. **Mental Health and Crisis Services**
Infinite Beginnings
526 E. Main St.
Lincolnton, NC 28092
704-748-4844

MONARCH/Mental Health
311 E. McBee Street
Lincolnton, NC 28092
704-732-1559 or 704-748-6113

Pathways MH/DD/SAS, LME-Gaston County
901 S. New Hope Rd.
Gastonia, North Carolina
704-867-2361

Phoenix Counseling Center
510 S. Aspen St.
Lincolnton, NC 28092
704-735-7710

2. **Substance Abuse Services**
Recovery Dynamics
326 E. Main St.
Lincolnton, NC 28092
704-735-3507

3. **Clothing/ Food Assistance/ Financial Services**
American Red Cross
(Emergency Assistance)
527 N. Aspen St.
Lincolnton, NC 28093
704-735-3500

Christian Ministry Lincoln County, Inc.
207 S. Poplar St.
Lincolnton, NC 28093
704-732-0383

Denver Wesleyan (By Appt.)
2391 North Hwy. 16
Denver, NC 28037
704-483-0469

East Lincoln Christian Ministry
4278 Catawba Buris Rd.
Denver, NC 28037
704-483-4415

Good Neighbor Shop
(Clothing)
116 S. Academy St.
Lincolnton, NC 28092
704-732-1835

WIC Clinic
704-736-8639

4. *Housing and Shelters*
Amy's House
(Domestic Violence)
Lincolnton, North Carolina
704-736-1224

Hesed House of Hope (Shelter)
100 Ann Gaither Circle
Lincolnton, NC 28092
704-732-0175

Lincolnton Housing Authority
806 McBee Street
Lincolnton, North Carolina
704-735-2221

United Way
(Housing Assistance)
P.O. Box 234
Lincolnton, North Carolina
704-732-8055

5. *Transportation*
Lincoln County Transportation
(TLC)
435 Salem Church Rd.
Lincolnton, NC 28092
704-479-2020 or 704-736-2030

Transportation Lincoln County
(Medicaid)
115 W. Main St.
Lincolnton, North Carolina
704-732-0738

6. *Medical Services*
Atrium Health
433 McAlister Rd.
Lincolnton, NC 28092
980-212-2000

Helping Hands Health Center
206 Gamble Dr., Suite C
Lincolnton, North Carolina
704-735-7145

Lincoln County
Health Department
200 Gamble Dr.
Lincolnton, NC 28092
704-735-3001 or 704-479-5030

**7. *Medication
Assistance Program***
GoodRx
855-26 8-2822

Lincoln County Department of
Social Services
1136 E. Main St.
Lincolnton, NC 28092
704-732-0738

Needy Meds
800-503-6897

8. *Employment/ Vocational Rehab/ Education*
Human Resources Department
115 W. Main St.
Lincolnton, NC 28092
704-736-8493

NC Cooperative
Extension Service
115 W. Main St.
Lincolnton, NC 28092
704-736-8452

NC Works Career Center
529 N. Aspen St.
Lincolnton, North Carolina
704-735-8035

9. *Legal Services*
Legal Aid of NC-
Gaston County
111 E. 3rd Ave., Suite 200
Gastonia, NC 28052
704-865-2357 or 800-230-5812

10. *Recreational/ Leisure*
Lincoln County Parks
and Recreation
302 N. Academy St.
Lincolnton, NC 28092
704-748-1518

Lincolnton Welcome Center
119 E. Water St.
Lincolnton, NC 28092
704-736-8980

11. *Special Populations*
Domestic Violence Coalition
Crisis Line 704-736-1224

Lincoln County Senior Center
612 Center Dr.
Lincolnton, NC 28092
704-732-9053

Salem Industries (Dev. Dis.)
1636 Salem Church Rd.
Lincolnton, North Carolina
704-732-1516

Veterans Services
302 N. Academy St.
Lincolnton, NC 28092
704-736-8506

CHAPTER 56

Macon County

1. **Mental Health and Crisis Services**
Appalachian
Community Services
100 Thomas Heights, Suite 206
Franklin, NC 28734
828-524-9385

Macon County Mental
Health Department
828-524-4435
VAYA Health
800-962-9003

2. **Substance Abuse Services**
Alcoholics Anonymous (AA)
828-254-8539

Poison Control Center
800-222-1222

3. **Clothing/ Food Assistance/ Financial Services**
CareNet
130 Bidwell St.
Franklin, NC 28734
828-369-2642

Emergency Food Assistance
Program (EFAP)
828-524-4617

WIC Program/Macon County
Public Health Center
828-349-2450 or 828-349-2453

4. **Housing and Shelters**
Macon County
Housing Department
23 Macon Avenue, Room 101
Franklin, NC 28734
828-369-2605

5. **Transportation**
Macon County Transit Services
5 W. Main St.
Franklin, NC 28734
828-349-2222

6. **Medical Services**
Macon County
Health Department
1830 Lakeside Dr.
Franklin, NC 28734
828-349-2081

7. *Medication*
    Assistance Program
    Macon County Department of
    Social Services
    1832 Lakeside Dr.
    Franklin, NC 28734
    828-349-2124

    Medication Assistance Program
    (MAP)
    828-349-6717 or 828-524-5258

8. *Employment/ Vocational*
    Rehab/ Education
    NC Works Career Center
    5 W. Main St.
    Franklin, NC 28734
    828-369-9534

9. *Legal Services*
    Legal Aid of North Carolina-
    Jackson County
    1286 W. Main St.
    Sylva, North Carolina
    828-586-8931 or 800-458-6817

10. *Recreational/ Leisure*
    Franklin Area Welcome Center
    98 Hyatt Rd.
    Franklin, NC 28734
    828-524-3161

11. *Special Populations*
    Macon County Senior Center
    108 Wayah Street
    Franklin, NC 28734
    828-349-2058

    Macon County
    Veterans Services
    104 E. Main St.
    Franklin, NC 28734
    828-349-2151

CHAPTER 57

Madison County

1. **Mental Health and Crisis Services**
RHA Behavioral
Health Services
13 S. Main St.
Marshall, NC 28753
828-649-9174

2. **Substance Abuse Services**
Madison Substance Awareness
Coalition (MSAC)
828-649-3531, extension 232

3. **Clothing/ Food Assistance/ Financial Services**
Beacon of Hope
120 Calvary Dr.
Marshall, NC 28753
828-649-3470

   Salvation Army
3421 US 25/70
Hot Springs, NC 28743
828-622-3355

4. **Housing and Shelters**
Community Housing Coalition
of Madison
798 Walnut Creek Rd.
Marshall, NC 28753
828-649-1200

   Marshall Housing Authority
630 N. Main St.
Marshall, NC 28753
828-649-2545

5. **Transportation**
Madison County
Transportation Authority
462 Longbranch Rd.
Marshall, NC 28753
828-649-2219

6. **Medical Services**
Madison County
Health Department
493 Medical Park Dr.
Marshall, NC 28753
828-649-3531

Mashburn Medical Center
590 Medical Park Dr.
Marshall, NC 28753
828-649-3500

7. **Medication
Assistance Program**
Madison County Department
of Social Services
5707 US Highway 25-70, Suite 1
Marshall, NC 28753
828-649-2711

Medication
Assistance Program/
Mashburn Medical Center
590 Medical Park Dr.
Marshall, NC 28753
828-649-3500

WNCAP – AIDS Project
828-252-7489

8. **Employment/ Vocational
Rehab/ Education**
NC Works/ (ESC)
4646 US Highway 25-70
Marshall, NC 28753
828-782-2632

9. **Legal Services**
Pisgah Legal Services
32 N. Main St.
Marshall, NC 28753
828-253-0406

10. **Recreational/ Leisure**
Madison County
Visitors Center
56 S. Main St.
Mars Hill, NC 28754
828-680-9031

11. **Special Populations**
Madison County Senior Center
356 N.W. US 25-70 Highway
Hot Springs, NC 28743
828-622-7427

CHAPTER 58

Martin County

1. **Mental Health and Crisis Services**
M-T-W Health Department
District-Washington County
198 NC Highway 45 N.
Plymouth, North Carolina
252-793-3023

   Tideland Mental Health
Center-Beaufort County
1308 Highland Dr.
Washington, North Carolina
252-946-8061

2. **Substance Abuse Services**
AA Hotline
252-975-6113 or 800-350-2538

   Trillium Health Resources-
Hertford County
144 Community College Rd.
Ahoskie, North Carolina
866-998-2597 or Hotline
877-685-2415

3. **Clothing/ Food Assistance/ Financial Services**
Catholic Charities
252-426-7717

   LCC Food Pantry
607 Washington St.
Williamston, North Carolina
252-792-8880

   Meals on Wheels
252-792-1027

   Salvation Army-
Beaufort County
112 E. 7th St.
Washington, NC 27889
252-946-2523

4. **Housing and Shelters**
Mid-East Regional
Housing Authority
415 East Blvd.
Williamston, NC 27892
252-789-4924

Options to Domestic Violence-
Beaufort County
Washington, North Carolina
252-940-1046

Robersonville
Housing Authority
106 N.W. Railroad Street
Robersonville, NC 27871
252-795-3134 or 252-217-2283

Shelter Home (Youth)
2295 Main St.
Jamesville, North Carolina
252-792-1883

Williamston Housing Authority
504 E. Main St.
Williamston, NC 27892
252-792-7571

Zion's Shelter and Soup Kitchen
(Men)-Beaufort County
102 W. 4th St.
Washington, NC 27889
252-975-1978

5. *Transportation*
Hinton's Employment
Transportation Services
252-802-4018 or 252-319-0025

Martin County Transit
305 E. Main St.
Williamston, NC 27892
252-789-4390

Medicaid Transportation
252-789-4460

6. *Medical Services*
Martin County
Health Department
210 W. Liberty St.
Williamston, NC 27882
252-792-7811

Martin Gen. Hospital
310 S. Mc Caskey Road
Williamston, NC 27892
252-792-2186

7. *Medication
Assistance Program*
Martin County Department of
Social Services
305 E. Main St.
Williamston, NC 27819
252-789-4400

MTW District
Health Department
201 W. Liberty St.
Williamston, NC 27892
252-793-1619

Rx Outreach
888-796-1234

8. *Employment/ Vocational
Rehab/ Education*
NC Works Career Center
407 East Blvd.
Williamston, NC 27892
252-792-7816

Vocational Rehabilitation
405 East Blvd.
Williamston, North Carolina
252-792-4033

9. *Legal Services*
   Legal Aid of
   NC-Hertford County
   Church Street
   Ahoskie, NC 27910
   252-332-5124 or 800-219-5262

   Legal Aid of NC- Pitt County
   301 Evans St., Suite 300
   Greenville, NC 27835
   252-758-0113

   Department of Juvenile Justice
   E. Main St.
   Williamston, NC 27892
   252-792-1382

10. *Recreational/ Leisure*
    Williamston Parks
    and Recreation
    300 Pine St.
    Williamston, NC 27892
    252-792-7042

    Martin County Travel
    &Tourism
    132 W. Main St.
    Williamston, NC 27892
    252-792-6605

11. *Special Populations*
    Martin County Adult Services
    222 E. Main St.
    Williamston, North Carolina
    252-792-1027

    Martin County Senior Center
    201 Lee St.
    Williamston, NC 27892
    252-792-1027

NC Head Injury Foundation
800-377-1464

Veteran Services
205 E. Main St.
Williamston, NC 27892
252-789-4398

CHAPTER 59

McDowell County

1. **Mental Health and Crisis Services**
McDowell County
Behavioral Health
5623 US 221
Glenwood, NC 28752
828-652-5444

McDowell Mental
Health Center
160 Spaulding Rd.
Marion, NC 28752
828-652-5837

RHA Behavioral Services-
Buncombe County
17 Church St.
Asheville, NC 28801
828-652-2919

2. **Substance Abuse Services**
Smoky Mountain Center LME/
MCO-Caldwell County
825 Wilkesboro
Blvd., Southeast
Lenoir, NC 28645
828-759-2160 or 800-849-6127

VAYA Health
408 Spaulding Rd., Suite B
Marion, NC 28752
800-849-6127

3. **Clothing/ Food Assistance/ Financial Services**
Foothills Food Hub
900 Baldwin Ave.
Marion, North Carolina
828-659-5289

Foothills Food Hub
7909 US 70
Nebo, North Carolina
828-659-5289

MANNA Food Bank
828-299-3663

Salvation Army (clothing)
828-659-2522

4. **Housing and Shelters**
Housing Voucher Program-
Rutherford County
111 W. Court St.
Rutherfordton NC 28139
828-748-0469

5. **Transportation**
Blue Hawk Transportation-
Anson County
710 Three Quarter Creek Rd.
Burnsville, NC 28714
828-536-5025

Faith Health NC of
McDowell County
828-738-4729

Here to There Transportation,
LLC (wheelchair)
Marion, NC 28752
828-317-8067

McDowell County Transit
300 Rockwell Dr.
Marion, NC 28752
828-559-0744

6. **Medical Services**
McDowell County
Health Department
408 Spaulding Rd.
Marion, NC 28752
828-652-6811

7. **Medication Assistance Program**
McDowell County Department
of Social Services
145 E. Court St.
Marion, NC 28752
828-652-3355

8. **Employment/ Vocational Rehab/ Education**
NC Division of
Vocational Rehabilitation
1170 W. Tate St.
Marion, NC 28752
828-652-2826

9. **Legal Services**
Legal Aid of NC-Foothills-
Burke County
211 E. Union St.
Morganton, NC 28655
828-437-8280

Pisgah Legal Services-
Buncombe County
Asheville, North Carolina
828-253-0406

10. **Recreational/ Leisure**
Blue Ridge Travelers'
Visitor Center
888-233-6111 or 800-VISIT NC

McDowell County
Visitor Center
91 S. Catawba Ave.
Old Fort, NC 28762
828-668-4282

11. *Special Populations*

McDowell County Domestic
Violence Victim
828-652-6150

McDowell County
Senior Center
100 Spaulding Rd.
Marion, NC 28752
828-659-0821

McDowell County
Veterans Services
100 Spaulding Rd.
Marion, NC 28752
828-652-2911

CHAPTER 60

Mecklenburg County

1. **Mental Health and Crisis Services**
Atrium Health Call Center
704-444-2400

Cardinal
Innovations Healthcare
800-939-5911

Mecklenburg Mental
Health, LME
429 Billingsley Rd.
Charlotte, North Carolina
704-336-2023

Monarch Crisis Services
866-272-7826

2. **Substance Abuse Services**
AA
704-332-4387 or 877-233-6853

Choices for Recovery
200 Queens Rd., Suite 102
Charlotte, NC 28204
980-280-1429

McLeod Centers for Well-being
500 Archdale Dr.
Charlotte, NC 28217
704-508-9515

Narcotics Anonymous
855-613-2762

Northstar Clinical Services
322 Lamar Ave., Suite #220
Charlotte, NC 28204
704-350-2485

3. **Clothing/ Food Assistance/ Financial Services**
Crisis Assistant Ministries
(Financial Assistance)
Charlotte, North Carolina
704-371-3000

Family Promise of Charlotte
2810 Providence Rd.
Charlotte, North Carolina
704-780-1624

Harvest Center-Food Pantry
1800 Brewton Dr.
Charlotte, NC 28206
704-333-4280

Heart and Hands-Food Pantry
202 S. Old Statesville Rd.
Huntersville, North Carolina
704-885-5828

Loaves and Fishes
14005 Stumptown Rd.
Huntersville, NC 28078
704-523-4333

Mallard Creek United House of
Prayer-Food Pantry
1739 Grace Ln.
Charlotte, NC 28262
704-547-1007

Salvation Army
11328 E. Independence Blvd.
Matthews, North Carolina
704-814-7031

Second Harvest Food Bank
500 Spratt St., #B
Charlotte, NC 28206
704-375-9639, extension 29

4. **Housing and Shelters**
Charlotte Housing Authority
135 Scaleybank Rd.
Charlotte, North Carolina
704-336-5183

Charlotte Rescue Mission
(Women in Recovery)
907 W. 1st St.
Charlotte, NC 28202
704-334-4935 or 704-333-4673

Oxford House (Men
in Recovery)
1318 Shamrock Dr.
Charlotte, North Carolina
704-344-1525

Salvation Army (Men
in Recovery)
1023 Central Ave.
Charlotte, North Carolina
704-322-1171

Urban Ministry Center
(Winter Shelter)
945 N. College St.
Charlotte, North Carolina
704-347-0278

Women's Shelter of Charlotte
1210 N. Tryon St.
Charlotte, North Carolina
704-334-3187

YWCA (Women)
3420 Park Rd.
Charlotte, North Carolina
704-525-5770

5. **Transportation**
Charlotte Area Transit System
(CATS)
600 E. 4th St.
Charlotte, NC 28202
704-336-7433

6. **Medical Services**
Mecklenburg County
Health Department
249 Billingsley Rd.
Charlotte, NC 28211
704-336-4700

7. **Medication Assistance Program**
GoodRx
855-268-2822

Mecklenburg County
Department of Social Services
301 Billingsley Rd.
Charlotte, NC 28211
704-336-3150

Needy Meds
800-503-6897

8. **Employment/ Vocational Rehab/ Education**
Charlotte JobLink
Career Center
5125 South Blvd., #A
Charlotte, NC 28217
704-527-3195

NC Works Career Center
8601 McAlpine Park Dr.,
Suite 110
Charlotte, NC 28211
704-566-2870

9. **Legal Services**
Legal Aid
1431 Elizabeth Ave.
Charlotte, North Carolina
704-971-2621 or 800-738-3868

10. **Recreational/ Leisure**
Charlotte Visitor
Information Center
329 S. Tryon St.
Charlotte, NC 28282
800-231-4636

Mecklenburg County Parks
and Recreation
5841 Brookshire Blvd.
Charlotte, NC 28216
980-314-1000

David B. Waymer Recreation
and Senior Center
14008 Holbrooks Rd.
Huntersville, NC 28078

Tourist Information Center
400 E. Martin Luther King
Jr. Boulevard
Charlotte, NC 28202

11. **Special Populations**
Autism Services
704-392-9220

Domestic Violence
National Hotline
800-799-7233

Levine Senior Center
1050 Devore Ln.
Matthews, NC 28105
704-846-4654

Mecklenburg County Crisis
(Support)
704-566-3410, option 1

Mecklenburg County
Veterans Services
320 S. Freedom Dr.
Suite 2000, Building D
Charlotte, NC 28208
704-336-2102

Mount Zion Senior Center
21445 Catawba Ave.
Cornelius, NC 28031
704-892-6031

North Meck Senior Center
102 Gilead Rd.
Huntersville, NC 28078
980-314-1127

Tyvola Senior Center
2225 Tyvola Rd.
Charlotte, NC 28210
980-314-1320

Veterans Homeless Program
877-424-3828

CHAPTER 61

Mitchell County

1. ***Mental Health and Crisis Services***
Western Highland Mental Health, LME- Buncombe County
356 Biltmore Avenue
Asheville, North Carolina
828-225-2800

2. ***Substance Abuse Services***
Vaya Health-Buncombe County
200 Ridgefield Ct.
Asheville, NC 28806
828-225-2785

3. ***Clothing/ Food Assistance/ Financial Services***
Friendship Baptist Church- Food Pantry
246 Baker Lane
Bakersville, NC 28705
828-208-0729

Salvation Army- Madison County
3421 NW US 25-70
Hot Springs, NC 28743
828-688-2104

Shepherd's Staff (Food Pantry)
6565 Highway 226 S.
Spruce Pine, NC 28777
828-765-5385

St. Lucian Catholic Church- Food Pantry
695 Summit Avenue
Spruce Pine, NC 28777
828-260-5982

Touch of Class (Clothes)
11885 **NC**-226, South
Spruce Pine, NC 28777
828-765-2704

WIC Clinic
828-688-2371 or 828-688-4668

4. **Housing and Shelters**
Hospitality House-
Watauga County
302 King St.
Boone, North Carolina
828-264-1237

Spruce Pine Public
Housing Authority
11 Fairgrounds St.
Spruce Pine, NC 28777
828-765-9182

Northwestern Regional
Housing Authority
828-688-3744

5. **Transportation**
Mitchell County
Transportation Authority
73 Crimson Laurel Way, #7
Bakersville, NC 28705
828-688-4715

6. **Medical Services**
Bakersville Health Center
86 N. Mitchelle Ave.
Bakersville, NC 28705
828-688-2104

Mitchell County
Health Department
1304 Service Dr., #A
Bakersville, NC 28705
828-688-6769 or 828-688-2371

7. **Medication Assistance Program**
Mitchell County Department of
Social Services
347 Long View Dr.
Bakersville, NC 28705
828-688-2175

8. **Employment/ Vocational Rehab/ Education**
NC Works Career Center/
Mayland Community College
200 Mayland Dr.
Spruce Pine, NC 28777
828-766-1195

9. **Legal Services**
Legal Aid-Watauga County
171 Grand Boulevard
Boone, North Carolina
828-264-5640 or 800-849-5666

Legal Aid of NC
828-437-8280

Legal Aid of
NC-Buncombe County
547 Haywood Rd.
Asheville, NC 28806
877-579-7562

10. **Recreational/ Leisure**
Mitchell County Visitor Center
79 Parkway Maintenance Road
Spruce Pine, NC 28777
828-765-9483

11. Special Populations

Mitchell SAFE PLACE
(Domestic Violence)
828-765-4015 or 877-765-4044
(Crisis Line)

Senior Center
26 Crimson Laurel Cir., Suite 2
Bakersville, NC 28705
828-688-2139

Veterans Service Officer
130 Forest Service Dr.
Bakersville, NC 28705
828-688-2200

CHAPTER 62

Montgomery County

1. **Mental Health and Crisis Services**
Day Mark Recovery Services
227 N. Main St.
Troy, NC 27371
910-517-3681

Sandhills Area Authority LME
910-673-9111

2. **Substance Abuse Services**
Day Mark Recovery Services
227 N. Main St.
Troy, NC 27371
910-517-3681

3. **Clothing/ Food Assistance/ Financial Services**
Second Harvest Food Bank
105 N. Main St.
Mount Gilead, NC 27306
910-439-4407

4. **Housing and Shelters**
Mount Gilead Housing
106 W. 2nd St.
Mount Gilead, NC 27306
910-898-9669

Star Housing
233 Center Street
Star, North Carolina
910-576-0611

Troy Housing Authority
408 S. Main St.
Troy, NC 27371
910-576-0611

5. **Transportation**
RCATS
444 N. Main St.
Troy, NC 27371
910-572-3430

6. **Medical Services**
Montgomery County
Health Department
217 S. Main St.
Troy, NC 27371
910-572-1339

7. *Medication Assistance Program*
Montgomery County
Department of Social Services
102 E. Spring St.
Troy, NC 27371
910-576-6531

8. *Employment/ Vocational Rehab/ Education*
NC Works Career Center
1011 Page St.
Troy, NC 27371
910-898-9669

9. *Legal Services*
Legal Aid of North Carolina-
Guilford County
122 N. Elm St., Suite 700
Greensboro, NC 27401
336-272-0148 or
866-8219-5262

10. *Recreational/ Leisure*
Discover Uwharrie
Welcome Center
100 W. Main St.
Troy, NC 27371
910-573-3153

Visitor Center
910-439-6802

11. *Special Populations*
Crisis Line (Domestic Violence)
910-572-3749

Montgomery County
Veterans Service
203 W. Main St.
Troy, NC 27371
910-576-4711

Troy Montgomery
Senior Center
200 Park Rd.
Troy, NC 27371
910-572-4464

CHAPTER 63

Moore County

1. ***Mental Health and Crisis Services***
Moore Free and
Charitable Clinic
211 Trimble Plant Road
Southern Pines, NC 28387
910-246-5333

   Sandhills Center for
Mental Health
1163 Seven Lakes Drive
West End, NC 27376
910-673-2972

2. ***Substance Abuse Services***
Crystal Lake and CASA works
285 Camp Easter Rd.
Lakeview, NC 28350
910-245-4339

   DayMark Recovery Services
205 Memorial Dr.
Pinehurst, NC 28374
910-295-6853

Port Human Services
206 N. Pine St.
Aberdeen, NC 28315
910-944-2189

3. ***Clothing/ Food Assistance/ Financial Services***
American Red Cross
115 Pennsylvania Ave.
Southern Pines, NC 28387
910-692-8571

   Carthage Food Pantry
108 Bruce St.
Carthage, NC 28327
910-245-4354

   Food Bank CENC
195 Sandy Ave.
Southern Pines, NC 28387
910-692-5959

4. ***Housing and Shelters***
Salvation Army
575 SE Broad Street
Southern Pines, NC 28387
910-725-1054

Southern Pines
Housing Authority
801 Mechanic St.
Southern Pines, NC 28387
910-692-2042

5. **Transportation**
Sandhills Moore Coalition for
Human Care
1500 Indiana Ave.
Carthage, NC 28387
910-693-1600

Moore County
Transportation Services
910-947-3389

6. **Medical Services**
Moore County
Health Department
705 Pinehurst Ave.
Carthage, NC 28327
910-947-3300

7. **Medication
Assistance Program**
Moore County Department of
Social Services
1036 Carriage Oaks Dr.
Carthage, NC 28327
910-947-2436

8. **Employment/ Vocational
Rehab/ Education**
North Carolina Vocational
Rehabilitation Services
150 Blake Blvd.
Pinehurst, NC 28374
910-295-1530

North Carolina Works
Career Center
245 Sheppard Trl.
Aberdeen, NC 28315
910-944-7697

9. **Legal Services**
Legal Aid of North Carolina-
Chatham County
959 East St.
Pittsboro, NC 27312
800-672-5834

10. **Recreational/ Leisure**
Moore County Visitors Center
155 W. New York Ave.,
Suite 300
Southern Pines, NC 28387
910-692-3330

11. **Special Populations**
Child Abuse Hotline
910-947-5683

Moore County Senior
Enrichment Center
8040 NC Hwy. 15-501
West End, NC 27376
910-215-0900

Services for the Blind
800-422-1897

Veterans Services
707 Pinehurst Ave
Carthage, NC 28327
910-947-3257

CHAPTER 64

Nash County

1. **Mental Health and Crisis Services**
Edgecombe-Nash Mental
Health Service/Eastpointe
500 Nash Medical Arts Mall
Rocky Mount, NC 27804
252-937-8141 or 888-893-8640

2. **Substance Abuse Services**
Coastal Playing Hospital and
Counseling Center
2301 Medpark Drive
Rocky Mount, NC 27804
252-962-5000 or 800-234-0234

Drug Education
Program/Rocky Mount
Police Department
331 S. Franklin St.
Rocky Mount, NC 27804
252-972-1436

3. **Clothing/ Food Assistance/ Financial Services**
A Touch of a Father's Love
Food Pantry
516 E. Nash St.
Spring Hope, NC 27882
252-377-2209

Faith Christian Ministries of
Nash County (Clothes)
245 W. Washington St.
Nashville, NC 27856
252-459-79 77

Helping Hands
136 Western Ave.
Rocky Mount, North Carolina
252-446-3340

Hobgood Citizens Group-
Halifax County
401 Beech St.
Hobgood, NC 27843
252-813-3126 or 252-279-8445

Meals on Wheels
153 N. Church St.
Nashville, NC 27856
252-459-1367

WIC Clinic
252-459-1325

4. **Housing and Shelters**
Catholic Charities
252-355-5111

My Sister's House (Shelter)
210 W. Washington St.
Nashville, NC 27856
252-641-6404

Rocky Mount
Housing Authority
1006 Aycock Street
Rocky Mount, North Carolina
252-977-3141

The Bassett Center Shelter
341 McDonald Street
Rocky Mount, North Carolina
252-985-1650

5. **Transportation**
Nash Edgecombe
Transportation Service (NETS)
252-937-6387

Rural General Public Program
(RGP)
100 Coastline St., Third Floor,
Suite 315
Rocky Mount, North Carolina
252-972-1517 or 252-972-1514

6. **Medical Services**
Nash County
Health Department
214 Barnes St.
Nashville, NC 27856
252-459-9819

7. **Medication Assistance Program**
Medigap
800-633-4227

Nash County Department of
Social Services
120 W. Washington St.,
Nashville, NC 27856
252-459-9831 or 252-459-9818

8. **Employment/ Vocational Rehab/ Education**
NC Division
Vocational Rehabilitation
301 S. Church St., Suite 100
Rocky Mount, NC 27804
252-977-2112

NC Works Career Center
793 Country Club Rd.
Rocky Mount, NC 27804
252-467-9300

Nash Edgecombe Wilson
Community Action Inc.
200 N. Church St.
Rocky Mount, NC 27802
252-442-8081 or 252-442-2580

9. **Legal Services**

Eastern Carolina Legal
Services Inc.
148 S. Washington St.
Rocky Mount, NC 27801
252-442-0635 or 866-219-5262

Legal Aid of NC
252-291-6851

10. **Recreational/ Leisure**

Nash County Tourist
Information Center
1104 Falls Rd.
Rocky Mount, NC 27804
252-972-5080

11. **Special Populations**

Child Abuse National Hotline
800-422-4453

My Sister's Home
(Domestic Violence)
252-462-0366 or 252-459-3094
(Crisis Line)

NC Head Injury Foundation
800-377-1464

Veterans Services
121 S. Fairview Rd.
Rocky Mount, North Carolina
252-446-2720

CHAPTER 65

New Hanover County

1. **Mental Health and Crisis Services**
   Coastal Horizon Center (Rape Crisis Center)
   Willie Stargell Office Park
   609 Shipyard Blvd., Suite 106
   Wilmington, NC 28412
   910-392-7185

   NHRMC Behavioral
   Health Hospital
   2131 S. 17th St.
   Wilmington, NC 28401
   800-451-9682

2. **Substance Abuse Services**
   Port Human Services
   1390 S. 16th St.
   Wilmington, NC 28401
   910-251-5326

   Trillium Health Resources
   3809 Shipyard Blvd.
   Wilmington, NC 28403
   866-998-2597 or (Crisis Line)
   877-685-2415

   Wilmington Treatment Center
   2520 Troy Dr.
   Wilmington, NC 28401
   910-762-2727, 855-912-6937,
   or 877-762-3750

3. **Clothing/ Food Assistance/ Financial Services**
   Breath of Life Ministries
   (Food Pantry)
   Arboretum Centre Building II
   5919 Oleander Dr., Suite 115
   Wilmington, NC 28403
   910-579-2828

   Food Bank of Central NC
   1314 Marstellar St.
   Wilmington, NC 28412
   910-251-1465, x 2204

   Helping Center of Federal Point
   (Food Pantry)
   Carolina Beach
   Recreation Center
   1121-B N. Lake Park Blvd.
   Carolina Beach, NC 28428
   910-458-2777

Helping Hands (Food Pantry)
St. Stanislaus Church
4849 Castle Hayne Rd.
Castle Hayne, NC 28429
910-452-6361

Martha's Kitchen
(Soup Kitchen)
409 N. Lake Park Blvd.
Carolina Beach, NC 28428
910-458-5134

Salvation Army
223 S. 3rd St.
Wilmington, NC 28402
910-762-7354

4. **Housing and Shelters**
Emergency Shelter
4938 Oleander Dr.
Wilmington, NC 28403
910-769-4730

First Fruit Ministries
(Domestic Violence)
2750 Vance St.
Wilmington, NC 28412
910-612-9438

Hopewood Supportive Housing
Program (Shelter)
2023 S. 17th St.
Wilmington, NC 28401
910-251-6440

Rescue Mission (Domestic
Violence Shelter)
502 Castle St.
Wilmington, North Carolina
910-343-0366

5. **Transportation**
Dial-A-Ride (DART)
910-202-2053

Wilmington Transit
Wave Authority
505 Cando St.
Wilmington, NC 28405
910-343-0106

6. **Medical Services**
New Hanover County
Community Health Center/
Med North
925 N. 4th St.
Wilmington, NC 28401
910-343-0270

New Hanover County
Health Department
2029 S. 17th St.
Wilmington, NC 28401
910-798-6500

7. **Medication
Assistance Program**
New Hanover County
Department of Social Services
1650 Greenfield St.
Wilmington, NC 28401
910-798-3400

Pharmacy Innovations
3608 Oleander Dr.
Wilmington, NC 28401
910-859-8211

8. ***Employment/ Vocational Rehab/ Education***
NC Works Career Center
1994 S. 17th St.
Wilmington, NC 28401
910-251-5777

NC Vocational
Rehabilitation Services
3340 Jaeckle Dr., Suite 201
Wilmington, NC 28403
910-251-5710

9. ***Legal Services***
Legal Services of Lower
Cape Fear
272 N. Front St., Suite 220
Wilmington, NC 28401
910-763-6207 or 866-219-5262

10. ***Recreational/ Leisure***
Community Arts Center
120 S. 2nd St.
Wilmington, NC 28401
910-341-7860

Parks and
Recreation Department
302 Willard St.
Wilmington, NC 28401
910-341-7855

USS North Carolina-Battleship
1 Battleship Road
Wilmington, NC 28401
910-399-9100

Wrightsville Beach
Visitor Center
305 W. Salisbury St.
Wrightsville Beach, NC 28480
910-256-8116

YMCA
11 S. Kerr Ave.
Wilmington, NC 28403
910-769-6800

11. ***Special Populations***
Autism Society of NC
4701 Wrightsville Ave.
Wilmington, North Carolina
910-332-0261

Disability Resource Center
910-815-6618

Division of Services for
the Blind
3240 Burnt Mill Drive, #7
Wilmington, NC 28403
910-251-5743

NC Division of Veterans Affairs
910-251-5704

New Hanover Senior Center
2222 S. College Rd.
Wilmington, NC 28403
910-798-6400

US Department of
Veterans Affairs
1705 Gardner Rd.
Wilmington, NC 28405
910-343-5300

CHAPTER 66

Northampton County

1. **Mental Health and Crisis Services**
ECU Health North Hospital-
Halifax County
250 Smith Church Road
Roanoke Rapids, NC 27870
252-535-8011

Roanoke- Chowan
Human Service (Referral)-
Hertford County
144 Community College Rd.
Ahoskie, North Carolina
252-332-4137

2. **Substance Abuse Services**
PORT Human Services-
Pitt County
4300 Sapphire Court, #110
Greenville, North Carolina
252-830-7540

3. **Clothing/ Food Assistance/ Financial Services**
CADA Food Pantry
120 Sessions Dr.
Rich Square, NC 27869
252-539-4155

Hannah's Closet (Clothes)-
Halifax County
1034 Roanoke Ave.
Roanoke Rapids, NC 27870
252-541-1127

WIC Clinic
252-534-5841

4. **Housing and Shelters**
Hannah's Place (Shelter)-
Halifax County
Roanoke Rapids,
North Carolina
252-537-2882

Roanoke- Chowan Regional
Housing Authority
205 Tinsley Way
Gaston, NC 27832
252-537-1051

Roanoke- Chowan Regional
Housing Authority
Rich Square, North Carolina
252-537-1051

Roanoke Rapids Housing
Authority-Halifax County
949 Roanoke Ave.
Roanoke Rapids, NC 27870
252-308-0693

Union Mission (Shelter)-
Halifax County
1310 Roanoke Ave.
Roanoke Rapids, NC 27870
252-537-3372

5. *Transportation*
Choanoke Public
Transportation Authority
505 N. Main St.
Rich Square, NC 27869
252-539-2022

6. *Medical Services*
Northampton County
Health Department
9495 NC Highway 305 N.
Jackson, NC 27845
252-534-5841

Rural Health Group-
Halifax County
717 S. Old Farm Rd.
Roanoke Rapids, NC 27870
252-536-5440

Vidant Roanoke-Chowan
252-209-3460

7. *Medication
Assistance Program*
Northampton County
Department of Social Services
9588 NC Highway 305
Jackson, NC 27845
252-534-5811

8. *Employment/ Vocational
Rehab/ Education*
NC Works Career Center-
Halifax County
1560 Julian R.
Allsbrook Highway
Roanoke Rapids, NC 27870
252-507-6180

9. *Legal Services*
Legal Aid of NC- Wake County
224 S. Dawson St.
Raleigh, NC 27601
866-219-5262

Legal Aid of NC
252-332-5124

10. *Recreational/ Leisure*
Northampton County
Recreation Department
P.O. Box 955
Jackson, NC 27845
252-534-1303

Northampton County
Visitors Center
127 W. Jefferson St.
Jackson, NC 27845
252-534-0331

11. *Special Populations*

JW Faison Senior Center
110 Ridgecrest Ln.
Jackson, NC 27845
252-532-1012

Roanoke Valley Adult Day
Center, Inc.-Halifax County
108 E. 1st St.
Weldon, NC 27890
252-536-2070

National Domestic
Violence Hotline
800-377-1464

Northampton County Veterans
Service Office
102 W. Jefferson St.
Jackson, NC 27845
252-534-2621

CHAPTER 67

Onslow County

1. **Mental Health and Crisis Services**
Brynn Marr Hospital
192 Village Dr.
Jacksonville, NC 28546
910-577-1400 or Hotline
910-577-1900

Dix Crisis Intervention Center
215-B Memorial Drive
Jacksonville, NC 28546
910-378-4809 or 866-437-1821

PORT Human Services
231 Memorial Dr.
Jacksonville, NC 28546
910-353-5354

2. **Substance Abuse Services**
Ala-non (AA)
215 Memorial Dr.
Jacksonville, NC 28580
910-353-4650

Jacksonville Treatment Center
806 Bell Fork Rd.
Jacksonville, North Carolina
910-347-2205

Substance Abuse Regional
Behavioral Health Services
(RHA)
215 Memorial Dr.
Jacksonville, North Carolina
910-353-4641 or 844-709-4097

Sunrise Group- St.
Anne's Church
711 Henderson Dr.
Jacksonville, NC 28540
910-347-3774

3. **Clothing/ Food Assistance/ Financial Services**
Goodwill (Clothes)
1113 Western Blvd.

Jacksonville, North Carolina
910-455-2025

Salvation Army
461 Center St.
Jacksonville, NC 28546
910-346-8800

WIC Services
910-347-2154

4. ***Housing and Shelters***
Catholic Charities
252-638-2188

Holly Regional
Housing Authority
910-329-6241

Onslow Community Outreach
(Shelter)
600 Court St.
Jacksonville, NC 28540
910-455-5733

Onslow County Women's
Center, Inc.
226 New Bridge St.
Jacksonville, NC 28540
910-347-4000

Second Chance Mission
(Shelter)
309 Court St.
Jacksonville, North Carolina
910-455-7111

5. ***Transportation***
Medical Van Service (Seniors)
4024 Richlands Hwy.
Jacksonville, NC 28540
910-455-2747

Onslow United Transit System
605 New Bridge St.
Jacksonville, NC 28540
910-346-2998 or 800-735-8262

6. ***Medical Services***
Caring Community Clinic
200 Doctors Dr., Suite B
Jacksonville, NC 28546
910-346-6149

Onslow County
Health Department
612 College St.
Jacksonville, NC 28540
910-347-2154

7. ***Medication
Assistance Program***
GoodRx
855-26 8-2822

Needy Meds
800-503-6897

Onslow County Department of
Social Services
1255 Hargett St.
Jacksonville, NC 28540
910-989-0230

8. ***Employment/ Vocational
Rehab/ Education***
NC Works Career Center
461 Western Blvd., Suite 106
Jacksonville, NC 28546
910-347-2121

Vocational Rehabilitation
39-B Office Park Drive
Jacksonville, NC 28546
910-455-1445

9. **Legal Services**
Legal Services of
NC-Wilmington
27 N. Front St., Suite 220
Wilmington, NC 28401
910-763-6207

10. **Recreational/ Leisure**
Holly Ridge Community Center
404 Sound Rd.
Holly Ridge, NC 28445
910-329-7081

Jacksonville
Tourism Development
815 New Bridge St.
Jacksonville, NC 28541
910-938-5200

Karen Beasley Sea
Turtle Rescue and
Rehabilitation Center
302 Tortuga Ln.
Surf City, NC 28445
910-329-0222

North Topsail Beach
Information Center
2008 Loggerhead Ct.
North Topsail Beach, NC 28460
910-328-1349

Northeast Creek Park
Crobin Road
Jacksonville, NC 28540
910-938-5314

Onslow County Tourism
1099 Gum Branch Road
Jacksonville, NC 28540
910-347-3141

Parks and Recreation
1244 Onslow Pines Rd.
Jacksonville, NC 28540
910-347-5332

Surf City Welcome Center
102 N. Shore Dr.
Surf City, NC 28445
910-328-2716

Swansboro Recreation Center
830 Main St., Ext.
Swansboro, NC 28584
910-326-2600

Wilson Gate Visitor Center
Camp Lejeune, North Carolina

11. **Special Populations**
Domestic Violence
Hotline-SAFE
800-799-7233

Oslow County Senior Services
4024 Richlands Hwy.
Jacksonville, NC 28540
910-455-2747

Senior Services
106 E. Franck St.
Richlands, NC 28574
910-324-1354

Sneads Ferry Senior Center
242 Sneads Ferry Rd.
Sneads Ferry, NC 28460
910-741-0670

Veterans Crisis Line
800-273-8255

CHAPTER 68

Orange County

1. **Mental Health and Crisis Services**
Alliance Health
800-510-9132

   ARC of Orange (for DD)
208 N. Columbia St.
Chapel Hill, North Carolina
919-942-5119

   Behavioral Health Clinic
919-956-4068

   Cardinal
Innovations Healthcare
201 Sage Rd.
Chapel Hill, North Carolina
800-939-5911

2. **Substance Abuse Services**
ADATC
919-575-7928

   Alcoholics Anonymous (AA)
919-933-0003

   Freedom House
Recovery Center
104 New Stateside Dr.,
Building 110
Chapel Hill, NC 27516
919-967-8844 or 866-275-9552

3. **Clothing/ Food Assistance/ Financial Services**
Amity United Methodist (Food Pantry/ Clothes Closet)
825 N. Estes Dr.
Chapel Hill, North Carolina

   IFC Food Pantry
919-929-6380, extension 2000

   Meals on Wheels
919-942-2948

   Orange CIM-Food Pantry
300 Millstone Dr.
Hillsborough, North Carolina
919-732-6194

4. **Housing and Shelters**
Cardinal Innovations (Shelter)
919-913-4144

Chapel Hill Department
of Housing
317 Caldwell St., Extension
Chapel Hill, North Carolina
919-968-2850

Interfaith Council –
Community House
(Male Shelter)
100 W. Rosemary St.
Chapel Hill, NC 27516
919-967-0643

Interfaith Council – Homestead
(Female Shelter)
2505 Homestead Road
Chapel Hill, NC 27516
919-932-6025

Orange County
Housing Authority
P.O. Box 8181
Hillsborough, NC 27278
919-245-2490

5. *Transportation*
Chapel Hill Transit
919-969-4900

EZ Rider (Disabled)
919-969-5544

Orange County
Public Transportation
919-245-2004

6. *Medical Services*
Orange County
Health Department
300 W. Tryon St.
Hillsborough, NC 27278
919-245-2411

Piedmont Health Services Inc.
182 Martin Luther King
Junior Boulevard
Chapel Hill, North Carolina
919-951-8741

7. *Medication
Assistance Program*
Orange County Department of
Social Services
300 W. Tryon St.
Hillsborough, NC 27278
919-245-2800

8. *Employment/ Vocational
Rehab/ Education*
NC Works
100 Europa Dr., Suite 101
Chapel Hill, North Carolina
919-245-4335

Orange County JobLink
Career Center
503 W. Franklin St.
Chapel Hill, North Carolina
919-969-3032

Vocational Rehabilitation
548 Smith Level Road
Carrboro, North Carolina
919-969-7350

9. ***Legal Services***
Legal Aid of
NC-Chatham County
959 East Street, Suite A & B
Pittsboro, North Carolina
919-542-0475

10. ***Recreational/ Leisure***
Chapel Hill/Orange County
Visitors Bureau
308 W. Franklin St.
Chapel Hill, NC 27516
919-245-4320

11. ***Special Populations***
Family Violence Prevention
Crisis Line-919-929-7122
Orange County Department
on Aging
919-968-2087

Orange Veteran Services Officer
300 W. Tryon St., 1st Floor
Hillsborough, North Carolina
919-245-2890

CHAPTER 69

Pamlico County

1. **Mental Health and Crisis Services**
News Mental Health Center-Craven County
1311 Health Dr.
New Bern, North Carolina
252-636-1510

   Still Waters Counseling
205 Main St.
Bayboro, North Carolina
252-745-4510

   Substance Abuse and Mental Health Service (SAMHSA) National Hotline
800-662-HELP

2. **Substance Abuse Services**
AA
252-633-3716

   Alcohol and Drug Abuse Crisis Line 252-637-7000

   New Beginnings
203 North St.
Bayboro, North Carolina
252-245-5760

   PORT Human Services-Pitt County
4300 Sapphire Ct., #110
Greenville, North Carolina
252-830-7540

3. **Clothing/ Food Assistance/ Financial Services**
Fishes and Loaves Pantry
Oriental, North Carolina
252-249-3687

   Hospice Thrift Store
602 Main St.
Bayboro, NC 28515
252-745-5033

   Pamlico County Disaster Relief Coalition
11560 NC Highway 855
Grantsboro, NC 28529
252-670-3413

Pamlico County ReStore
14172 NC Highway 55, West
Bayboro, NC 28515
252-745-1106

Reelsboro Methodist Church
252-745-3266

Salvation Army (Food)
13708 NC Highway 55, South
Alliance, NC 28509
252-745-3828

Salvation Army (Clothing)
13704 NC Highway 55
Bayboro, NC 28515
252-745-3528

4. **Housing and Shelters**
Catholic Charities-
Craven County
252-638-2188

Coastal Women's Shelter-
Craven County
1333 S. Glen Bernie Rd.
New Bern, NC 28560
252-638-4509 or 252-638-5995

5. **Transportation**
CARTS-Craven County
252-636-4917

6. **Medical Services**
Craven County
Health Department
203 North St.
Bayboro, NC 28515
252-745-5111

Pamlico Medical Center
606 Main St.
Bayboro, North Carolina
252-745-3191

7. **Medication Assistance Program**
GoodRx
855-268-2822

NeedyMeds
800-503-6897

Pamlico County Department of
Social Services
828 Alliance Main St.
Bayboro, NC 28515
252-745-4086 or 252-745-4046

8. **Employment/ Vocational Rehab/ Education**
Pamlico Career Center
252-631-9525

Pamlico County
Workforce Center
705 Main St.
Bayboro, NC 28515
252-745-9934

9. **Legal Services**
Legal Aid of NC-Pitt County
301 Evans St., Suite 102
Greenville, NC 27858
252-758-0113 or 866-219-5262

10. *Recreational/Leisure*
Pamlico County Chamber
of Commerce
10642 NC Highway 55, East
Grantsboro, NC 28529
252-745-3008

Pamlico County Parks
and Recreation
202 Main Street
Bayboro, NC 28515
252-745-4240

11. *Special Populations*
NC Victim Services
800-826-6200

Pamlico County Senior Services
800 Main St.
Alliance, NC 28509
252-745-3488 or 252-745-7196

Veterans Service Office
Courthouse Annex, #210
Bayboro, North Carolina
252-745-3925

Veteran Services
828 Alliance Main St.
Bayboro, NC 28515
252-745-4086

CHAPTER 70

Pasquotank County

1. **Mental Health and Crisis Services**
Albemarle Mental Health Center
Elizabeth City, North Carolina
252-335-0803

Albemarle Regional Health Services
711 Roanoke Ave.
Elizabeth City, NC 27909
252-335-5914 or 252-338-4400

Kids First, Inc.
Child Abuse Treatment Center
1825 W. City Dr.
Elizabeth City, NC 27909
252-338-5658

PORT Human Services
1141 N. Road St., Suite L
Elizabeth City, NC 27909
252-335-5914

2. **Substance Abuse Services**
Alcoholics Anonymous
252-256-0580

Mental Health/Substance Abuse Program
252-335-0801

Pathways Counseling Center
508 E. Main St., Suite 201
Elizabeth City, NC 27909
252-338-5334

3. **Clothing/ Food Assistance/ Financial Services**
Albemarle Food Pantry, Inc.
6679 W. Guadalupe St.
Elizabeth City, NC 27906
252-335-4035

Camden Food Pantry-Camden County
197 Highway 343, South
Camden, NC 27921
252-335-7565

Food Bank of Albemarle
109 Tidewater Way
Elizabeth City, NC 27909
252-335-4035

Goodwill
502 W. Ehringhaus Street
Elizabeth City, NC 27909
252-562-6610

New Life Family Center
(Food Pantry)
400 E. Elizabeth St.
Elizabeth City, NC 27909
252-333-1202

Salvation Army-Food Pantry
602 N. Hughes Blvd.
Elizabeth City, NC 27909
252-338-4129

Tabernacle of Faith Community
Outreach Center (Food Pantry)
1300 Walker Ave.
Elizabeth City, NC 27909
252-338-7705

WIC Clinic
252-338-4400

4. **Housing and Shelters**
Catholic Charities-
Perquimans County
Hertford, North Carolina
252-426-7717

Economic Improvement
Council, Inc.
104 W. Airing House St.
Elizabeth City, NC 27909
252-338-5338

Elizabeth City
Housing Authority
440 Hariot Dr.
Elizabeth City, NC 27909
252-335-5411

Hope House
(Domestic Violence)
252-335-5493

Independent Living Program
401 S. Griffin St.
Elizabeth City, NC 27909
252-338-0175

The Garden of Hope House
(Women Shelter)
508 S. Road Street
Elizabeth City, NC 27909
252-335-0080

5. **Transportation**
Inter-County Public
Transit Authority
110 Kitty Hawk Ln.
Elizabeth City, NC 27909
252-338-4480

6. **Medical Services**
Community Care Clinic
918 Greenleaf St.
Elizabeth City, NC 27909
252-384-4733

Pasquotank County
Health Department
711 Roanoke Ave.
Elizabeth City, NC 27909
252-338-4400

7. **Medication Assistance Program**
NeedyMeds
800-503-6897

Pasquotank County
Department of Social Services
709 Roanoke Ave.
Elizabeth City, NC 27906
252-338-2126

8. **Employment/ Vocational Rehab/ Education**
NC Works/Job Link Center
422 N. McArthur Dr.
Elizabeth City, NC 27909
252-331-4798

Vocational
Rehabilitation Services
401 S. Griffin St., Suite 100
Elizabeth City, NC 27909
252-331-4798

9. **Legal Services**
Legal Aid of
NC-Hertford County
610 E. Church St.
Ahoskie, NC 27910
252-332-5124

10. **Recreational/ Leisure**
Elizabeth City Welcome Center
606 E. Main St.
Elizabeth City, NC 27909
252-335-5330

Knobbs Creek
Recreation Center
200 E. Ward St.
Elizabeth City, NC 27909
252-335-1424

Mariner's Wharf Park
508 S. Water St.
Elizabeth City, NC 27909
252-338-8128

YMCA
1240 N. Road Street
Elizabeth City, NC 27909
252-334-9622

11. **Special Populations**
Elizabeth City Senior Center
200 E. Ward St.
Elizabeth City, NC 27909
252-337-6661

Veterans Services Office
1023 US Highway 17, South
Elizabeth City, North Carolina
252-331-4741

West lawn Memorial Park
(Cemetery)
1909 W. Main St.
Mount Herman,
North Carolina
252-338-3931

CHAPTER 71

Pender County

1. **Mental Health and Crisis Services**
Anchor Psychological
and Counseling
16581 US Hwy 17, Suite 600
Hampstead, NC 28443
910-270-9995

Coastal Care MH/DD/SA
Services-New Hanover County
3809 Shipyard Blvd.
Wilmington, North Carolina
910-550-2600

Trillium Health Resources
877-685-2415

2. **Substance Abuse Services**
Alcoholics Anonymous-New
Hanover County
5001 Wrightsville Ave.
Wilmington, NC 28435
910-794-1840

Christian Drug Detox
341-11 College Rd., Suite 2041
Wilmington, NC 28425
910-794-1840

Coastal Horizons Center
803 S. Walker St.
Burgaw, NC 28425
910-259-0668 or Crisis Line
800-672-2903

3. **Food Assistance/ Financial Services**
Catholic Charities
Harrelson Center
20 N. 4th St., Suite 300
Wilmington, NC 28401
910-251-8130

Food Bank of Central Carolina-
New Hanover County
1314 Marstellar St.
Wilmington, NC 28402
910-251-1465

Livingstone Tabernacle
127 Sloop Point Rd.
Hampstead, NC 28443
910-270-0750

Pender County
Christian Services
210 W. Fremont St.
Burgaw, NC 28425
910-259-5840

WIC Clinic
910-259-1230

We Care 4 U Foundation
8910 US Highway 117, North
Watha, NC 28478
910-300-7014

4. Housing and Shelters

Cape Fear Area Housing
Crisis Hotline
910-444-4998

Domestic Violence Shelter-New
Hanover County
Wilmington, North Carolina
910-343-0703

Pender County
Housing Authority
505 E. Satchwell St.
Burgaw, North Carolina
910-259-1343

Pender County
Housing Department
805 S. Walker St.
Burgaw, NC 28425
910-259-1208

Safe Haven Women's Domestic
Violence Shelter
Burgaw, North Carolina
Hotline 910-259-8989

5. Transportation

who will weird but anyway
DSS-Medicaid Transportation
910-259-1375

Pender Adult Services
(PAS TRANS)
910-259-9119

6. Medical Services

Maple Hill Medical Center
4811 NC Highway 50
Maple Hill, NC 28454
910-259-6659

Pender County
Health Department
803 S. Walker St.
Burgaw, NC 28425
910-259-1230

Pender County
Health Department-
Hampstead Annex
1506 US Highway 17
Hampstead, NC 28443
910-270-6704

Women's Health Clinic-New
Hanover County
24 S. 17th St.
Wilmington, NC 28401
910-851-5011

7. Medication Assistance Program

GoodRx
855-268-2822

NeedyMeds
800-503-6897

Pender County Department of
Social Services
810 S. Walker St.
Burgaw, NC 28425
910-259-1240

8. **Employment/ Vocational
   Rehab/ Education**
   NC Division of
   Vocational Rehabilitation
   P.O. Box 1099
   Burgaw, North Carolina
   910-259-0159

   Pender Career Center/Job Link
   904 S. Walker St.
   Burgaw, NC 28425
   910-259-0240

9. **Legal Services**
   Legal Aid of NC
   201 N. Front St., Suite 220
   Wilmington, NC 28401
   910-763-6207

   Magistrate's Court
   104 N. Walker St.
   Burgaw, NC 28425
   910-663-3919

10. **Recreational/ Leisure**
    Parks and
    Recreation Department
    805 S. Walker St.
    Burgaw, NC 28425
    910-399-1030

    Topsail Beach Parks
    and Recreation
    820 S. Anderson Blvd.

Topsail Beach, NC 28445
910-328-1560

Visitors Center
106 E. Wilmington St.
Burgaw, NC 28425
910-259-1278

11. **Special Populations**
    Interface Refugee Ministry
    (Migrants/Refugees)
    252-633-9009

    Pender Adult Services (Seniors)
    901 S. Walker St.
    Burgaw, NC 28425
    910-259-9119

    Services for the Blind
    Burgaw, North Carolina
    910-259-1464

    Veteran's Administration
    108 S. Cowan Street
    Burgaw, NC 28425
    910-259-1203

    Veterans Services
    805 S. Walker St.
    Burgaw, North Carolina
    910-207-2526

CHAPTER 72

Perquimans County

1. **Mental Health and Crisis Services**
Albemarle Mental Health Center/ PORT-Pasquotank County
1141 N. Road St.
Elizabeth City, NC 27909
252-335-0803

East Carolina Behavioral Health- Hertford County
144 Community College Rd.
Ahoskie,NC 27910
252-332-4137

2. **Substance Abuse Services**
AA-Pasquotank County
Elizabeth City, North Carolina
252-338-1849

PORT Health Services-Pasquotank County
1141 N. Road St.
Elizabeth City, NC 27909
252-335-0803

3. **Clothing/ Food Assistance/ Financial Services**
Christ Temple Holiness Church
5058 Highway 11 N.
Bethel, NC 27812
252-757-3671

Food Bank of the Albemarle-Pasquotank County
109 Tidewater Way
Elizabeth City, NC 27909
252-335-4035

Goodwill Clothing
502 W. Ehringhaus St.
Elizabeth City, NC 27909
252-562-6610

New Life Family Center-Food Pantry
400 E. Elizabeth St.
Elizabeth City, NC 27909
252-333-1202

Salvation Army
602 N. Hughes Blvd.
Elizabeth City, NC 27909
252-338-4129

WIC Clinic
252-426-2100

4. **Housing and Shelters**
Albemarle Hopeline (
Domestic Violence Shelter)-
Pasquotank County
Elizabeth City, North Carolina
252-338-3011

Hertford Housing Authority
104 White St.
Hertford, NC 27944
252-426-5663

5. **Transportation**
Inter-County Public
Transit Authority
110 Kitty Hawk Ln.
Elizabeth City, NC 27909
252-338-4480

6. **Medical Services**
Community Care Clinic-
Pasquotank County
918 Greenleaf St.
Elizabeth City, NC 27909
252-384-4733

Perquimans County
Health Department
103 ARPDC Street
Hertford, NC 27944
252-426-2100

7. **Medication
Assistance Program**
Perquimans County
Department of Social Services
103 Charles St.
Hertford, NC 27944
252-426-7373

8. **Employment/ Vocational
Rehab/ Education**
NC Works Career Center-
Pasquotank County
422 N. McArthur Dr.
Elizabeth City, NC 27909
252-331-4798

Vocational
Rehabilitation Services
401 S. Griffin St., Suite 100
Elizabeth City, NC 27909
252-331-4768

9. **Legal Services**
Legal Aid of NC-
Hertford County
610 E. Church St.
Ahoskie, NC 27910
252-332-5124

10. **Recreational/ Leisure**
Perquimans County
Visitor's Center
104 Dobbs St.
Hertford, NC 27944
910-409-8021

11. **Special Populations**
National Domestic
Violence Hotline
252-426-1796

Perquimans County
Senior Center
1072 Harvey Point Rd.
Hertford, NC 27944
252-426-5404

Veteran Services
104 Dobbs St.
Hertford, NC 27944
252-426-1796

CHAPTER 73

Person County

1. **Mental Health and Crisis Services**
Person Family Medical/Dental/
Behavioral Health
702 N. Main St.
Roxboro, NC 27573
336-599-9271

   VAYA Health
   800-849-6127

2. **Substance Abuse Services**
Freedom House
Recovery Center
336-599-8366

3. **Clothing/ Food Assistance/ Financial Services**
Safe Haven of Person
P.O. Box 624
Roxboro, NC 27573
910-597-8699

   Word Life Food Pantry
   704 Franklin St.
   Roxboro, NC 27573
   336-322-0488

4. **Housing and Shelters**
Roxboro Housing Authority
500 Mount Bethel Church Rd.
Roxboro, NC 27573
336-599-8616

   Roxboro Section 8
   Housing Office
   808 Lyle St.
   Roxboro, NC 27573
   336-322-3111

5. **Transportation**
Person Area Transportation
System (PATS)
336-599-7484

6. **Medical Services**
Person County
Health Department
355-A S. Madison Blvd.
Roxboro, NC 27573
336-597-2204

7. **Medication Assistance Program**
American Pharmacist Association
800-237-2742

Person County Department of Social Services
355-B S. Madison Blvd.
Roxboro, North Carolina
336-599-8361

8. **Employment/ Vocational Rehab/ Education**
Vocational Rehabilitation
157 Semora Rd.
Roxboro, NC 27573
336-597-2150

9. **Legal Services**
Legal Aid of
NC-Durham County
201 W. Main St., Suite 400
Durham, North Carolina
919-688-6396

10. **Recreational/ Leisure**
Person County Visitor Center
705 Durham Rd.
Roxboro, NC 27573
336-597-2689

11. **Special Populations**
Indian Affairs
141 N. Madison St.
Roxboro, NC 27573
336-599-0952

National Domestic
Violence Hotline
800-799-7233

NC 4 VETS
919-807-4250

Person Veteran Services Officer
216 W. Barden St.
Roxboro, NC 27573
336-597-7891

Safe Haven of Person County
119 S. Main St.
Roxboro, North Carolina
336-599-7233

CHAPTER 74

Pitt County

1. **Mental Health and Crisis Services**
Care Counseling
108 Oakmont Dr.
Greenville, NC 27858
252-355-2801

ECU Psychiatry
Outpatient Clinic
905 John Hopkins Dr.
Greenville, NC 27834
252-744-1406

Pitt County Mental
Health Center
203 Government Cir.
Greenville, North Carolina
252-413-1600

Port Human Services
4300 Sapphire Ct., #110
Greenville, North Carolina
252-830-7540

Trillium Health Resources
201 W. 1st St.
Greenville, NC 27834
877-685-2415

2. **Substance Abuse Services**
AA
252-758-0787

Flynn Christian
Fellowship Home
4035 Roundtree Rd.
Ayden, NC 28513
252-756-5022

Narcotics Anonymous
252-758-0787

Walter B Jones Alcohol
and Drug Abuse
Rehabilitation Center
2577 W. 5th St.
Greenville, NC 27834
252-830-3426

3. **Clothing/ Food Assistance/ Financial Services**
Ayden Christian Care Center
(Emergency Food)
4106-B West Avenue
Ayden, NC 27513
252-746-2995

Bethel Methodist Church
(Emergency Food)
3798 James St.
Bethel, NC 27812
252-825-8041

Food Bank of Central
Eastern NC
1712 Union St.
Greenville, NC 27834
252-752-4996

Hope of Glory
103 E. Arlington Blvd.,
Suite 106
Greenville, NC 27858
252-227-4684

Salvation Army
2337 W. Dickenson Ave.
Greenville, NC 27834
252-756-3388

WIC Program
252-902-2393

4. **Housing and Shelters**
Ayden Housing Authority
4316 Liberty St.
Ayden, NC 27813
252-746-2021

Catholic Charities
252-355-5111

Community Crossroad Center
207 Manhattan Ave.
Greenville, NC 27834
252-752-0829

Farmville Housing Authority
4284 Anderson Ave.
Farmville, NC 27828
252-753-5347

Greenville Housing Authority
1103 Broad Street
Greenville, NC 27834
252-329-4000

Oxford House-Men (Recovery)
2521 S. Memorial Dr.
Greenville, North Carolina
252-756-1616

Oxford House-Women
(Recovery)
112 W. 12th St.
Greenville, North Carolina
252-752-3976

Ronald McDonald House
(Families of hospital-
ized children)
529 Moye Boulevard
Greenville, NC 27834
252-847-5435

5. **Transportation**
Greenville Area Transit
(GREAT)
1500 Beauty St.
Greenville, NC 27834
252-329-4532

Pitt Area Transit System (PATS)
252-902-2980

6. *Medical Services*
Pitt County Health Department
201 Government Cir.
Greenville, NC 27834
252-902-2449 or 252-902-2300

Vidant Medical Center
2100 Stantonburg Rd.
Greenville, NC 27834
252-847-4100

7. *Medication*
Assistance Program
GoodRx
855-268-2822

Pitt County Department of
Social Services
1717 W. 5th St.
Greenville, NC 27834
252-902-1110 or 252-902-1064

8. *Employment/ Vocational*
Rehab/ Education
Eastern Carolina
Vocational Center
901 Staton Rd.
Greenville, NC 26831
252-758-4188 or 800-758-4188

Job Corps
252-355-9067

NC Division of
Vocational Rehabilitation
101 Fox Haven Dr.
Greenville, NC 27858
252-830-8560

NC Works Career Center
3101 Bismark St.
Greenville, NC 27834
252-355-9069

9. *Legal Services*
Legal Aid of North Carolina
301 S. Evans, Suite 102
Greenville, NC 27835
252-758-0113

10. *Recreational/ Leisure*
Department of Parks
and Recreation
2000 Cedar Ln.
Greenville, NC 27858
252-329-4567

Greenville Visitors Bureau
417 Cotanche St., #100
Greenville, NC 27858
252-329-4200

Winterville Recreation Park
332 Sylvania St.
Winterville, NC 28590
252-756-1487

11. *Special Populations*
Autism Society of NC Inc.
2045 Eastgate Dr., Suite C
Greenville, NC 27858
919-756-1819

Cancer Services of Eastern NC
252-561-5351

Carolina's Poison Center
800-222-1222

Center for Family
Violence Prevention
(Domestic Violence)
Crisis Line-252-752-3811

Greenville VA Health
Care Center
4011 Moye Blvd.
Greenville, NC 27834
252-830-2149

Grifton Senior Center
101 Creek Shore Dr.
Grifton, NC 28530
252-524-5072

PICASO (AIDS)
1530 Evans St., Suite 106
Greenville, NC 27834
252-830-1660

Services for the Blind
404 Saint Andrews Dr.
Greenville, NC 27834
252-355-9016 or 800-422-1877

Veteran's Services
1717 W. 5th St.
Greenville, NC 27834
252-902-3090

Veterans Services
200 Eastbrook Dr., #A
Greenville, North Carolina
252-830-6395

CHAPTER 75

Polk County

1. **Mental Health and Crisis Services**
Life Span Psychological Services
Columbus, North Carolina
828-894-2300

2. **Substance Abuse Services**
New Hope Counseling
Columbus, North Carolina
828-894-8101

3. **Clothing/ Food Assistance/ Financial Services**
Thermal Belt Outreach
Ministry Food Pantry
134 White Dr.
Columbus, NC 28722
828-894-2988

WIC Clinic
828-894-8271 or 894-3888

4. **Housing and Shelters**
Catholic Charities
800-227-7261

Community
Assistance Program
500 Carolina Dr.
Tryon, NC 28782
828-859-5560

Housing Assistance
214 N. King St.
Hendersonville, NC 28792
828-692-4744

Polk County Housing Authority
(Town Hall)
113 Ashley Meadows Cir.
Columbus, NC 28722
828-894-8236

5. **Transportation**
Polk County Transportation
Courthouse Annex Building 3
Columbus, NC 28722
828-894-8203

6. **Medical Service**
   Polk County
   Health Department
   161 Walker St.
   Columbus, NC 28722
   828-894-8271

7. **Medication Assistance Program**
   Polk County Department of Social Services
   231 Wolfverine Trl.
   Mill Spring, NC 28756-4501
   828-894-2100

   Department of Social Services
   330 Carolina Dr.
   Tryon, NC 28782
   828-859-5825

8. **Employment/ Vocational Rehab/ Education**
   Polk County
   Vocational Rehabilitation
   Columbus, North Carolina
   828-894-3041

   Rutherford County Job Link (ESC)
   139 E. Trade St.
   Forrest City, NC 28043
   828-245-9841

9. **Legal Services**
   Legal Aide-Buncombe County
   184 E. Chestnut St.
   Asheville, North Carolina
   828-236-1080

   Legal Aid of North Carolina
   866-219-5262

   Pisgah Legal Services-Buncombe County
   Asheville, North Carolina
   828-253-0406

10. **Recreational/ Leisure**
    First Peak of the Blue Ridge
    Visitor Center
    20 E. Mills St.
    Columbus, NC 28722
    828-894-2324

11. **Special Populations**
    Children's
    Developmental Services
    704-480-5440

    Polk County Veterans Services
    75 Carmel Ln.
    Columbus, NC 28722
    828-894-0003

CHAPTER 76

Randolph County

1. **Mental Health and Crisis Services**
Asheboro Psychiatric Services
723 S. Cox St.
Asheboro, NC 27203
336-629-9139

Randolph Counseling Center
505 S. Church St.
Asheboro, NC 27203
336-625-3888

Suicide Prevention Lifeline
800-273-8255

2. **Substance Abuse Services**
DayMark Recovery Services
110 W. Walker Ave.
Asheboro, NC 27205
336-633-7000

DayMark Recovery Services
205 Balfour Dr.
Archdale, NC 27263
336-431-0700

North Carolina Division
of Mental Health and
Developmental Disabilities and
Substance Abuse (MH/DD/SA)
984-236-5000

3. **Clothing/ Food Assistance/ Financial Services**
Our Daily Bread Soup Kitchen
831 E. Pritchard St.
Asheboro, NC 27203
336-626-2563

Ramseur Food Pantry
724 Liberty St.
Ramseur, North Carolina
336-824-8045

Salvation Army
345 N. Church St.
Asheboro, NC 27205
336-625-0551

United Way
363 S. Cox St.
Asheboro, NC 27205
336-625-4207

WIC Program
336-318-6171

4. **Housing and Shelters**
Asheboro Housing Authority
338 W. Wainman Ave.
Asheboro, NC 27203
336-629-4146

Randleman Housing Authority
606 S. Main St.
Randleman, NC 27317
336-498-7686

Room at the Inn
135 Sunset Avenue
Asheboro, North Carolina
336-625-1500

5. **Transportation**
RCATS
347-B W. Salisbury St.
Asheboro, NC 27203
336-629-7433

PART (to Greensboro)
336-662-0002

One Hundred Men (to
Chapel Hill)
336-622-5774

6. **Medical Services**
Randolph County
Health Department (Ira
McDowell Center)
2222-B S. Fayetteville St.
Asheboro, NC 27205
336-318-6200

7. **Medication
Assistance Program**
Randolph County Department
of Social Services
1512 N. Fayetteville St.
Asheboro, NC 27204
336-683-8000

8. **Employment/ Vocational
Rehab/ Education**
NC Works Career Center
600 S. Fayetteville St.
Asheboro, NC 27205
336-625-5128

North Carolina Division of
Vocational Rehabilitation
958 S. Park St.
Asheboro, NC 27203
336-629-1040

9. **Legal Services**
Legal Aid-Guilford County
122 N. Elm St.
Greensboro, North Carolina
336-272-0148 or 800-951-2257

10. **Recreational/ Leisure**
NC Visitors Center
(I-73/74 Southbound)
4393 Interstate
73/74 Northbound
Seagrove, NC 27341
336-873-7213

North Carolina Zoo
4401 Zoo Pkwy.
Asheboro, NC 27205
800-488-0444

Visitor Center
2858 Parks X Roads
Church Road
Ramseur, North Carolina
336-824-1031

11. *Special Populations*
Family Prices Center
(Domestic Violence)
336-629-4159

Hope4 NC Helpline
855-587-3463

NC4Vets
844-624-8387

Randolph County Veterans
Services (Shaw Building)
158 Worth St.
Asheboro, NC 27205
336-318-6909

Randolph Senior Center
347 W. Saulsberry St.
Asheboro, NC 27205
336-625-3389

CHAPTER 77

Richmond County

1. **Mental Health and Crisis Services**
Behavioral Health Crisis Line
833-600-2054

   DayMark Recovery Services
116 S. Lawrence St.
Rockingham, NC 28379
910-895-2462

   Sandhills Alternative Academy
(adolescences)
121 Pine Needle Ln.
Hamlet, NC 28345
910-417-4922

   Sandhills Alternative Academy
(adolescences)
503 Rocking Ham Rd.
Rockingham, NC 28379
910-417-4922

   Sandhills Behavioral Care, LME
523 Rockingham Rd.,
Rockingham, NC 28379
910-562-9882 or 800-256-2452

2. **Substance Abuse Services**
DayMark Recovery Services
523 US-1 North
Rockingham, NC 28379
910-719-4335

3. **Clothing/ Food Assistance/ Financial Services**
Helping Hands of Hamlet
615 Cheraw Road
Hamlet, North Carolina
910-334-1009

   Our Daily Bread
106 S. Randolph St.
Rockingham, North Carolina
910-895-3536

4. **Housing and Shelters**
Hamlet Housing Authority
1104 Fisher Ave.
Hamlet, North Carolina
910-997-3316

   Rockingham Housing
809 Armistead St.
Rockingham, North Carolina
910-997-3316

5. **Transportation**
Area of Richmond Transit
(ART)
125 Caroline St.
Rockingham, North Carolina
910-895-1313

6. **Medical Services**
Richmond County
Health Services
127 Caroline St.
Rockingham, NC 28379
910-997-8301

7. **Medication
Assistance Program**
Richmond County Department
of Social Services
125 Caroline St.
Rockingham, NC 28379
910-997-8400

8. **Employment/ Vocational
Rehab/ Education**
NC Works
115 W. Franklin St.
Rockingham, North Carolina
910-997-9180

North Carolina
Vocational Rehabilitation
1793 E. Broad Ave.
Rockingham, North Carolina
910-997-9230

9. **Legal Services**
Legal Aid-Chatham County
959 East St.
Pittsboro, North Carolina
919-542-0 475-4800-672-5834

10. **Recreational/ Leisure**
Hamlet Visitors Center
14 W. Main St.
Hamlet, North Carolina
910-582-0603

Richmond County
Visitor Center
101 W. Broad Ave.
Rockingham, NC 28379
910-895-9057

11. **Special Populations**
Ellerbe Senior Center
306 Millston Road
Ellerbe, North Carolina
910-652-6006

Girl Scouts
NC Coastal Times
800-284-4475

Hamlet Senior Center
102 Veterans Dr.
Hamlet, North Carolina
910-582-7985

Hoffman Senior Center
267 Blues Bridge Rd.
Hoffman, North Carolina
910-281-5957

New Horizons (Domestic
Violence) Crisis line
910-997-4840

Rockingham Senior Center
225 S. Lawrence St.
Rockingham, North Carolina
910-997-4491

Veterans Service Officer
1401 Fayetteville Rd.
Rockingham, North Carolina
910-997-8232

CHAPTER 78

Robeson County

1. **Mental Health and Crisis Services**
Eastpointe/Monarch Outpatient Mental Health Services
2003 Goodwin Ave., Suite C
Lumberton, NC 28358
866-272-7826

Monarch Facility Based Crisis
207 W. 29th St.
Lumberton, NC 28358
910-618-5606

RHA Health Services
2003 Goodwin Ave., Suite A-1
Lumberton, NC 28358
910-739-8849

Southeastern Family Violence and Rape Crisis Center
215 E. 3rd St.
Lumberton, NC 28358
252-739-6278

Southeastern Regional Mental Health, LME
450 Country Club Rd.
Lumberton, NC 28360
910-738-5261

2. **Substance Abuse Services**
Lifebridge Drug and Substance
2501 E. Elizabeth Rd.
Lumberton, NC 28360
910-738-7880

Lumberton Treatment Center
2200 Clayborn Church Rd.
Lumberton, NC 28360
910-739-9160

Non-Hospital
Medical Detoxification
2003 Goodwin Ave., Suite C
Lumberton, NC 28358
910-674-4814

3. ***Clothing/ Food Assistance/***
Financial Services
American Red Cross
600 W. 5th St.
Lumberton, NC 28358
910-738-5057

Caring Touch Outreach
799 James Lynn Rd.
Pembroke, NC 28372
910-521-9175

Clothing and Such (Clothes)
3842 NC Highway 41, South
Fairmont, NC 28340
910-628-5444

Emergency Rental and
Utility Assistance
910-521-7861

Four-County Community
Services-Cumberland County
435 Caton Rd.
Fayetteville, NC 28360
910-277-3500

Old Prospect United Methodist
Church- Food Bank
3929 Missouri Rd.
Maxton, NC 28364
910-521-2111

Partners in Ministry
12 3rd St.
Lawrenceburg, NC 28352
910-277-3377

Robeson County Church
and Community Center
(Clothing Assistance)
600 W. 5th St.
Lumberton, NC 28358
910-738-5204

Sacred Pathways
303 W. College St.
Pembroke, NC 28372
910-521-2685

WIC Clinic
910-671-3274

4. ***Housing and Shelters***
Fairmont Housing Authority
910-628-7467

Lumberton Christian
Care Shelter
305 E. 1st St.
Lumberton, NC 28352
910-739-1204

Lumberton Housing Authority
910-671-8200

Our House (Pregnant Women)
910-521-1464
Pembroke Housing Authority
606 Lumbee St.
Pembroke, NC 28372
910-521-9711

Robeson County
Housing Authority
100 Oxendine Cir.
Lumberton, NC 28360
910-738-4866

5. **Transportation**
Southeast Area Transit System
1519 Carthage Rd.
Lumberton, NC 28358
910-618-5679

6. **Medical Services**
Robeson County
Health Department
460 Country Club Rd.
Lumberton, NC 28360
910-671-3200

Southeastern Regional
Medical Center
300 W. 27th St.
Lumberton, NC 28360
910-671-5000

7. **Medication
Assistance Program**
Robeson County Department
of Social Services
435 Caton Rd.
Lumberton, NC 28360
910-671-3500

NeedyMeds
800-503-6897

8. **Employment/ Vocational
Rehab/ Education**
NC Works Career Center/
JobLink
289 Corporate Dr., Suite B
Lumberton, NC 28352
910-618-5500

Southeastern Industrial Center
430 Caton Rd.
Lumberton, NC 28360
910-738-8138

Vocational
Rehabilitation Services
289 Corporate Dr., #A
Lumberton, NC 28358
910-618-5513 or 910-618-5518

9. **Legal Services**
Legal Aid of NC
101 E. 2nd St.
Pembroke, NC 28372
910-521-2831

Robeson County Court House
Clerk of Court
500 N. Elm St.
Lumberton, NC 28360
910-272-3100

10. **Recreational/ Leisure**
Lumberton Visitors Center
3431 Lackey St.
Lumberton, NC 28360
910-739-9999

Pembroke Recreation Complex
7164 NC Highway 71
Pembroke, NC 28372
910-521-7182

11. **Special Populations**
Guardian ad litem Program
435 Caton Rd.
Lumberton, NC 28360
910-671-3077

Lumbee Tribe of NC
6984 Highway 711, West
Pembroke, NC 28372
910-521-7861

Robeson County AIDS
Task Force
123 W. 4th St.
Lumberton, NC 28358
910-618-0090

Robeson County
Veteran's Services
113 W. 8th St.
Lumberton, NC 28358
910-671-3071

CHAPTER 79

Rockingham County

1. **Mental Health and Crisis Services**
Cone Health Outpatient Behavioral Health
621 S. Main St., #200
Reidsville, NC 27320
336-349-4454

Rockingham County Mental Health Department
128 Deer Trail Road
Reidsville, NC 27320
336-342-1611

2. **Substance Abuse Services**
DayMark Recovery Services
355 County Home Rd.
Reidsville, NC 27320
336-342-8316

3. **Clothing/ Food Assistance/ Financial Services**
Reidsville Outreach Center
435 S.W. Market St.
Reidsville, NC 27320
336-342-7770

Reidsville Soup Kitchen
336-349-5701

Rockingham Red Cross Food Pantry
3692 NC-14
Reidsville, NC 27320
336-349-3434

4. **Housing and Shelters**
Madison Housing Authority
925 Fern St.
Madison, NC 27025
336-548-6619

Reidsville Housing Authority
924 3rd Ave.
Reidsville, NC 27320
336-589-6510

5. **Transportation**
Department of Transportation
425 NC 65
Reidsville, NC 27320
336-342-8138

ADTS/ RCATS
336-349-2343

6. **Medical Services**
   Public Health Department
   371 NC Highway 65
   Reidsville, NC 27320
   336-342-8140

7. **Medication Assistance Program**
   Rockingham County
   Department of Social Services
   411 NC Highway 65
   Wentworth, NC 27375
   336-342-1394

8. **Employment/ Vocational Rehab/ Education**
   Joblink/NC Works
   8340 NC 87
   Reidsville, NC 27320
   336-634-5600

   Work First
   336-342-1394

9. **Legal Services**
   Legal Assistance Program-
   Durham County
   201 W. Main St., Suite 400
   Durham, NC 27701
   866-219-5262

   NC Guardian Ad
   Litem Program
   336-634-6107

10. **Recreational/ Leisure**
    Reidsville Visitor Center
    140 S. Scales St.
    Reidsville, NC 27320
    844-230-3040

11. **Special Populations**
    Help, Inc. (Domestic Violence)
    336-342-3331

    Mental Help Crisis Line
    (CPHS)
    888-581-9988

    Senior Citizen Center
    201 N. Washington Ave.
    Reidsville, NC 27320
    336-394-1088

    Veterans Services
    405 NC Highway 65
    Reidsville, NC 27320
    336-342-8449

CHAPTER 80

Rowan County

1. ***Mental Health and Crisis Services***
Lifeworks Behavioral Health
612 Mocksville Avenue, #2
Salisbury, NC 28144
704-210-5302

    Piedmont Behavioral Health,
LME-Cabarrus County
245 Le Phillip Court
Concord, North Carolina
704-721-7000

2. ***Substance Abuse Services***
DayMark Recovery Services
2129 Statesville Boulevard
Salisbury, NC 28147
704-633-3616

3. ***Clothing/ Food Assistance/ Financial Services***
Grateful Heart
Community Service
706 Dunns Mountain Rd.
Granite Quarry, North Carolina
704-202-9226

Helping Hands Food Pantry
Bethel Baptist Church
1209 ¼ Opal Street
Kannapolis, North Carolina
704-933-2125

Main Street Mission
306 S. Main St.
China Grove, NC 28023
704-855-2909

Meals on Wheels
704 – 633 – 0352

Rockwell Church of God
607 China Grove Hwy.
Rockwell, North Carolina
704-279-0658

Rowan Helping Ministries
785 Grampian Rd.
Mount Ulla, North Carolina
704-637-6838

Salvation Army
620 Bringle Ferry Rd.
Salisbury, NC 28144
704-636-6491

WIC Clinic
704-216-8777, ext.4

4. **Housing and Shelters**
Dayspring
214 S. Main St.
Salisbury, NC 28144
704-638-8915

East Spencer
Housing Authority
704-637-2284

Rowan Housing Authority
310 Longmeadow Dr.
Salisbury, North Carolina
704-633-8380

Salisbury Housing Authority
200 S. Boundary St.
Salisbury, North Carolina
704-636-1410

United Way-Rowan County
704-633-1802

5. **Transportation**
North Carolina Department
of Transportation
4770 S. Main St.
Salisbury, NC 28147
704-630-3200

Rowan Transit
704-630-0981 or 704-216-8888

6. **Medical Services**
Rowan County
Health Department
1813 E. Innes St.
Salisbury, NC 28146
704-216-8777

7. **Medication Assistance Program**
MAP – C/O Community
Care Clinic
315 – G Mocksville Avenue
Salisbury, NC 28144
800-662-7030 or 704-636-4523

Rowan County Department of
Social Services
1813 E. Innes St.
Salisbury, NC 28144
704-216-8330

8. **Employment/ Vocational Rehab/ Education**
JobLink Center/ ESC
1904 S. Main St.
Salisbury, NC 28144
704-639-7529

Vocational Rehabilitation Office
323 N. Main St.
Salisbury, NC 28144
704-639-7575

9. **Legal Services**
Legal Aid-Guilford County
122 N. Elm St.
Greensboro, North Carolina
336-272-0148

10. **Recreational/ Leisure**
Rowan County Visitors Center
204 E. Innes St.
Salisbury, NC 28144
704-638-3100

11. Special Populations

Rowan County Senior Services
1120 A. Boundary Street
Salisbury, NC 28144
704-636-2344

Rowan County Senior
Services Department
704-216-7700

Rowan County Veterans
Service Office
1935 Jake Alexander Blvd. W.,
Suite A – 2
Salisbury, NC 28147
704-216-8138

CHAPTER 81

Rutherford County

1. Mental Health and Crisis Services

Family Preservation Services
of NC
356 Charlotte Rd.
Rutherfordton, NC 28139
828-288-2707

ONASS Place All in One
Dayhab Treatment Facility
115 W. Court St., Suite B
Rutherfordton, NC 28139

RHA Health Services
132 Commercial Dr., Suite 120
Forrest City, NC 28043
828-248-1117

Rutherford Regional
Health System-Behavioral
Health Services
288 S. Ridgecrest Ave.
Rutherfordton, NC 28139

2. Substance Abuse Services

Alcoholics Anonymous
Rutherfordton
Presbyterian Church
252 N. Washington St.
Rutherfordton, NC 28139
828-287-3466

Blue Ridge Counseling
202 E. Main St.
Springdale, NC 28160
828-286-0501

Out of Ashes Ministry
(Recovery Refuge)
131 Countryside Dr.
Forrest City, NC 28043
828-395-2000

Recovery Road/Element
Church (Support Group)
1071 S. Broadway St.
Forrest City, NC 28043
828-245-7766

United Way of Rutherford County (Support Groups)
668 Withrow Rd.
Forrest City, NC 28043
828-286-3929

3. *Clothing/ Food Assistance/ Financial Services*
Chase Corner Ministries-Food Pantry
1604 Chase High Road
Forrest City, NC 28043
828-247-0096

Graham Town Community Center
129 1st St.
Forrest City, NC 28043
828-229-3380

Meals on Wheels (Seniors)
828-287-6409

Neighbors Pantry Inc.
217 Gilkey School Rd.
Rutherfordton, NC 28139
828-652-5437

New Beginnings Suit Kitchen
668 N. Washington St.
Rutherfordton, NC 28139
828-286-9278

Salvation Army
256 W. Main St.
Forrest City, NC 28043
828-287-0119

Washburn Community Outreach Center
2934 Piney Mountain Church Rd.
Bostic, NC 28018
828-245-5603

Yokefellow Service Center (Emergency Assistance)
132 Blanton Street
Springdale, NC 28160
828-287-0776 (by appointment)

WIC Clinic
828-287-6238

4. *Housing and Shelters*
Forrest City Housing Authority
147 E. Spruce St.
Forrest City, NC 28043
828-245-1390

Grace of God Rescue Mission (Emergency Shelter)
537 W. Main St.
Forrest City, NC 28043
828-245-9141

Hope Network of Rutherford County (Transitional Housing-Women)
1071 S. Broadway St.
Forrest City, NC 28043
828-367-4673

Path Shelter/Family Resources of Rutherford County
828-245-8595 (Domestic Violence Crisis Line)

5. **Transportation**
Rutherford County Transit
294 Fairground Road
Spindale, NC 28160
828-287-6339

Rutherford County Transit
Medical Appointments
828-287-6141

6. **Medical Services**
Blue Ridge Community
Health Center
187 W. Main St.
Spindale, NC 28160
828-692-4289

Blue Ridge Health
Lake Lure, NC 28746
828-625-4400

Rutherford County
Health Department
221 Callahan Koon Rd.
Spindale, NC 28160
828-287-6100

7. **Medication
Assistance Program**
Rutherford County Department
of Social Services
389 Fairground Rd.
Spindale, NC 28160
828-287-6199

Rutherfordton
Medication Assistance
828-288-8872

8. **Employment/ Vocational
Rehab/ Education**
NC Employment
Security Commission
139 E. Trade St.
Forrest City, NC 28043
828-245-9841

NC Vocational Rehabilitation
227 Commercial Dr.
Forrest City, NC 28043
828-245-1223

NC Works Career Center
223 Charlotte Rd.
Rutherfordton, NC 28139
828-286-3042

9. **Legal Services**
Pisgah Legal Services
169 N. Main St.
Rutherfordton, NC 28139
828-247-0297

Pisgah Legal Services-
Buncombe County
184 E. Chestnut St.
Asheville, NC 28802
828-236-1080

10. **Recreational/ Leisure**
Callison Recreation Center
217 Clay St.
Forrest City, NC 28043
828-248-5220

Kiwanis Park
Green Street
Rutherfordton, NC 28139
828-287-3523

Rutherford Outdoor Coalition
115 N. Oak St.
Spindale, NC 28160
828-351-3235

Spindale House
119 Tanner St.
Spindale, NC 28160
828-286-3716

11. *Special Populations*
Family Resources
(Domestic Violence)
Crisis Line 828-245-8595

Hands of Hope for Life
(Pregnant Women)
129 N. Powell St.
Forrest City 28043
828-247-4673

Lifeline (Emergency Services)
828-286-5673

Rutherford County
Senior Center
193 Callahan-Koon Rd.
Spindale, NC 28160
828-287-6409

Rutherford County
Veteran Services
303 Fairground Rd.
Spindale, NC 28160
828-287-6185

Rutherfordton Lions Club
(Eyewear Assistance)
828-429-2209

CHAPTER 82

Sampson County

1. ***Mental Health and Crisis Services***
Alternative Care Treatment Systems (ACTS)
207 W. Main St.
Clinton, NC 28328
910-592-1202

CommWell Health-
Building Bridges
417 Vance St.- Unit B
Clinton, NC 28328
910-567-7107

Eastpointe Human
Services, LME
800-913-6109

Sampson County Crisis Center
309 E. Main St.
Clinton, NC 28328
910-592-3599

2. ***Substance Abuse Services***
AA
45 Godwin Farm Ln.
Clinton, NC 28328
800-350-2538

Angelic House (Women)
405 County Complex Rd.
Clinton, NC 28328
910-567-5020

Hope of Sampson
51 Rowan Road
Clinton, NC 28328
910-590-0100

Sampson County Narcotics
1341 Lisbon St.
Clinton, NC 28328
910-592-8917

3. ***Clothing/ Food Assistance/ Financial Services***
Action Pathways/Second
Harvest Food Bank
360 County Complex Rd.
Clinton, NC 28329
910-485-6131 or 800-758-6923

Enlighten the World Ministries
(Clothes)
P.O. Box 231
Roseboro, NC 28382
910-260-4336 or 877-366-3646

First Baptist Church
(Soup Kitchen)
900 College St.
Clinton, NC 28328
910-592-2883

Revival Deliverance Center, Inc.
(Food)
101 E. Pinewood St.
Roseboro, NC 28382
910-990-0967

WIC Department-
Sampson County
910-592-1131

4. **Housing and Shelters**
Eastern Carolina Regional
Housing Authority
313 Barden St.
Clinton, NC 28328
910-289-2750 or 910-592-3129

Eastern Carolina Regional
Housing Authority
200 Brantwood Cir.
Roseboro, NC 28382
910-525-4193

First Baptist Homeless Shelter
820 College St.
Clinton, NC 28328
910-592-4658

5. **Transportation**
Sampson Area Transportation
Services (SAT)
311 County Complex Rd.
Clinton, NC 28328
910-299-0127

6. **Medical Services**
Sampson County
Health Department
360 County Complex Rd.
Building E, Suite 200
Clinton, NC 28328
910-260-4336

Sampson Medical Group
301 Main St.
Newton Grove, NC 28366
910-594-0046

7. **Medication
Assistance Program**
GoodRx
855-268-2822

NeedyMeds
800-503-6897

Sampson County Department
of Social Services
360 County Complex Rd.,
Suite 100
Clinton, NC 28328
910-592-7131

8. **Employment/ Vocational
Rehab/ Education**
N.C. Works Career Center
115 North Blvd.
Clinton, NC 28328
910-592-5756

Sampson County Vocational
Rehabilitation Services
215 W. Main St.
Clinton, NC 28328
910-592-4051

9. **Legal Services**

Legal Aid of NC (LANC)-
Cumberland County
327 Dick St., Suite 103
Fayetteville, NC 28301
910-483-0400

Legal Aid of
NC-Johnston County
300 S. 3rd St., Suite 371
Smithfield, NC 27577
866-219-5262

10. **Recreational/ Leisure**

Sampson County Convention
and Visitors Bureau
414 Warsaw Rd.
Clinton, NC 28328
910-592-2557

Sampson County Parks
and Recreation
405 County Complex Rd.
Building B, Suite 130
Clinton, NC 28328
910-299-0924

Spivey's Corner Wiffle Ball
Miffly Field
Spivey's Corner, NC 28334

The Center for Health
and Wellness
417 E. Johnson St.
Clinton, NC 28328
910-596-5400

11. **Special Populations**

Garland Senior Center
91 N. Church Ave.
Garland, NC 28441
910-529-3931

NC Commission of
Indiana Affairs
7531 N. US 421 Highway
Clinton, NC 28328
910-564-6152 or 910-564-6909

Roseboro Senior Center
206 NE. Railroad St.
Roseboro, NC 28382
910-525-5706

Sampson County Department
of Aging
371 Rowan Rd.
Clinton, North Carolina
910-592-4653

Sampson County Veteran's
Service Office
119 W. Main St.
Clinton, NC 28328
910-592-2862

CHAPTER 83

Scotland County

1. ***Mental Health and Crisis Services***
Advantage Behavioral Health
405 Biggs St.
Laurinburg, NC 28352
910-610-4444

Eastpointe MCO
Crisis Line – 800-913-6109

Grief Support Group
610 Lauchwood Dr.
Laurinburg, NC 28352
910-276-7176

MONARCH
103-B McAlpine Lane
Laurinburg, NC 28352
910-277-2663 or 800-568-9689
(Crisis Line)

RHA Behavioral Health
1779 S. Main St.
Laurinburg, NC 28352
910-277-3212

2. ***Substance Abuse Services***
Alcoholics Anonymous
800-350-2538

Generations Health
Services, LLC
911 Atkinson St.
Laurinburg, NC 28352
910-291-9909

National Institute on
Drug Abuse
Hotline – 800-662-HELP

Scotland Family
Counseling Center
601-B Lauchwood Drive
Laurinburg, NC 28352
910-276-7011

3. ***Clothing/ Food Assistance/ Financial Services***
American Red Cross
227 S. Main St.
Laurinburg, NC 28352
910-276-0600

Gift Love Food Pantry
17881 St. John's Church Road,
#B
Laurel Hill, NC 28351

Helping Hands (Clothing)
130 Biggs St.
Laurinburg, NC 28352
910-276-3090

Partners in Ministry
12 3rd St.
East Laurinburg, NC 28352
910-277-3355

Restoring Hope Center
1106 N. Main St.
Laurinburg, NC 28352
910-276-4460

Spring Hill Baptist-Food Pantry
24220 Main St.
Wagram, NC 28396
910-369-2335

WIC Clinic
910-277-2440

4. **Housing and Shelters**
Laurinburg Housing Authority
1300 Woodlawn Dr.
Laurinburg, NC 28352
910-276-3439

Scotland County Concerning
Citizens for the Homeless
130 Biggs St.
Laurinburg, NC 28353
910-276-8420

5. **Transportation**
Scotland County Transit System
(SCATS)
1403-C West Boulevard
Laurinburg, NC 28353
910-227-2416

6. **Medical Services**
Scotland County Community
Health Clinic (Free Clinic)
1405-B West Boulevard
Laurinburg, NC 28352
910-277-9912

Scotland County
Health Department
1405 West Blvd.
Laurinburg, NC 28352
910-277-2440

7. **Medication
Assistance Program**
GoodRX
855-268-2822

NeedyMeds
800-503-6897

Scotland County Department
of Social Services
1405 West Blvd.
Laurinburg, NC 28352
910-277-2500

8. **Employment/ Vocational
Rehab/ Education**
Department of
Vocational Rehabilitation
915-D S. Main St.
Laurinburg, NC 28352
910-276-3894 or 910-276-4669

NC Works Career Center/ ESC
303 N. Main St.
Laurinburg, NC 28352
910-276-4260

9. **Legal Services**
Legal Aid of NC-Lumberton
County's
101 E. 2nd St.
Pembroke, NC 28372
910-521-2831

10. **Recreational/ Leisure**
Beacham Park
300 S. Austin St.
Maxton, NC 28364
Gipson Park
6281 Highway 79
Gipson, NC 28343
910-277-2411

Hamlet Visitors Center-
Richmond County
14 Main St.
Hamlet, NC 28345
910-582-0603

Scotland County Parks
and Recreation
1206 Turnpike Road
Laurinburg, NC 28352
910-277-2585

Scotland County Tourism
Development Authority
507 W. Covington St.
Laurinburg, NC 28353
910-277-3149

11. **Special Populations**
Domestic Violence Crisis Line
910-276-6268 or 800-739-8622

Lumbee Tribe of North
Carolina- Robeson County
6984 NC Highway 711
Pembroke, NC 28372
910-521-7861

National
Alzheimer's Association
Hotline – 800-272-3900

Scotland County Civic
Senior Center
1210 Turnpike Road
Laurinburg, NC 28352
910-277-2550

Veteran's Services Office
507 W. Covington St.
Laurinburg, NC 28352
910-277-2597

CHAPTER 84

Stanly County

1. **Mental Health and Crisis Services**
Atrium Health-
Behavioral Health
301 Yadkin St.
Albemarle, NC 28001
980-323-4000 or 980-323-4492

Atrium Health Psychiatry
& Counseling
923 N. 2nd St., Suite 105
Albemarle, NC 28001
704-403-1877

2. **Substance Abuse Services**
DayMark Recovery Services
1000 N. 1st St., Suite 1
Albemarle, NC 28801
704-983-2117

3. **Clothing/ Food Assistance/ Financial Services**
Norwood Church of God-
Food Pantry
130 W. Pine St.
Norwood, NC 28128
704-474-3328

PGBC Food Pantry
Frog Pond Road
Oakboro, NC 28129

Providence Church-
Food Pantry
12474 NC 24-27 Highway
Locust, NC 28097
704-888-5697

South Davidson Family
Resource Center-
Davidson County
292 S. Main St.
Denton, NC 27239
336-859-5399

TB2G Food Pantry-
Cabarrus County
11000 Reed Mime Road
Midland, NC 28107
704-786-4700

WIC Clinic
704-986-3003

4. **Housing and Shelters**
Albemarle Housing Authority
300 S. Bell Ave.
Albemarle, North Carolina
704-984-9580

Gaston Community Action
507 Old Charlotte Rd.
Albemarle, NC 28001
704-985-1928

5. **Transportation**
Stanly County Umbrella
Services Agency (SCUSA)
1000 N. 1st St., Suite 15
Albemarle, NC 28001
704-986-3790

6. **Medical Services**
Stanl's y County
Health Department
1000 N. 1st St., #3
Albemarle, NC 28001
704-982-9171

Community Care Clinic
303 Yadkin St., Suite C
Albemarle, NC 28001
980-323-4668

7. **Medication Assistance Program**
Stanly County Department of
Social Services
1000 N. 1st St., Suite 2
Albemarle, NC 28001
704-982-6100

8. **Employment/ Vocational Rehab/ Education**
NC Works Career Center
944 N. 1st St.
Albemarle, NC 28001
704-982-2183

Vocational Rehabilitation
702 Henson St.
Albemarle, NC 28001
704-982-8124

9. **Legal Services**
Legal Aide-Cabarrus County
785 Davidson Dr., NW
Concord, North Carolina
704-786-4145 or 800-849-8009

10. **Recreational/ Leisure**
New London Memorial Park
220 N. Main St.
New London, NC 28127
704-463-5423

Richfield Community Park
245 Hwy. 49, North
Richfield, NC 27137
704-463-1308

Stanly County Visitors Bureau
1000 N. 1st St.
Albemarle, NC 28001
704-986-2583

11. Special Populations

Crisis Council
(Domestic Violence)
704-985-1981

Stanly County Senior Center
283 N. 3rd St.
Albemarle, NC 28001
704-986-3769

Veterans Services
Stanly Commons
1000 N. 1st St., Suite 6
Albemarle, NC 28001
704-986-3694

CHAPTER 85

Stokes County

1. **Mental Health and Crisis Services**
Community Corrections
1011 Main St.
Danbury, NC 27016
336-593-2441

   Pioneer Community Hospital
of Stokes Behavioral Health
336-593-8281

   Sid's House
530 N. Main St.
Walnut Cove, NC 27052
252-542-9333

2. **Substance Abuse Services**
VAYA Health
3172 NC Highway 8, South
Unit B
Walnut Cove, NC 27052
800-849-6127

   Stokes County Medicaid
Addiction Treatment Center
522 N. Main St.
Walnut Cove, NC 27052
888-744-9884

3. **Clothing/ Food Assistance/ Financial Services**
Stokes County Food Pantry
221 Ingram Dr.
King, NC 27021
336-983-4357

   Northern Stokes Food Pantry
7257 NC Highway 89
Westfield, NC 27053
336-351-0900

   WIC Program
336-593-2402

4. **Housing and Shelters**
Stokes County
Rental Assistance
Walnut Cove Public Library
106 W. 5th St.
Walnut Cove, NC 27052
336-904-0334

5. **Transportation**
Medicaid Transportation
1014 Main St.
Danbury, NC 27016
336-593-2811

Yadkin Valley
Public Transportation
336-679-2071

6. **Medical Services**
Stokes County
Health Department
1009 Main St.
Danbury, NC 27016
336-593-2400

7. **Medication
Assistance Program**
Stokes County Department of
Social Services
1010 Main St.
Danbury, NC 27016
336-593-2861

8. **Employment/ Vocational
Rehab/ Education**
Job Link Center-Stokes County
506 S. Main St.
Walnut Cove, NC 27052
336-591-4074

Stokes County
Vocational Rehabilitation
Highway 89
Danbury, NC 27016
336-593-9444

9. **Legal Services**
Legal Aid of North Carolina
336-75-9162

10. **Recreational/ Leisure**
Hanging Rock State Park
Visitor Center
1790 Hanging Rock Park Rd.
Walnut Cove, NC 27052
336-593-8480

Stokes County Visitor Center
Third Floor -Ronald
Reagan Building
1014 Main St.
Danbury, NC 27016
336-593-2496

11. **Special Populations**
Veterans Services
1012 Main St.
Danbury, NC 27016
336-593-2468 or 336-593-2811

Walnut Cove Senior Center
308 Brooke St.
Walnut Cove, NC 27052
336-591-5442

CHAPTER 86

Surry County

1. Mental Health and Crisis Services
Crossroads Behavioral Health
200 Business Park
Elkin, North Carolina
336-835-1000

New River Behavioral Health
847 Westlake Dr.
Mount Airy, NC 27080
336-783-6919

2. Substance Abuse Services
DayMark Recovery Services
40 W. Lebanon St.
Mount Airy, NC 27030
336-783-6919

Salvation Army
651 S. South Street
Mount Airy, NC 27030
336-786-4075

3. Clothing/ Food Assistance/ Financial Services
East Duplin Christian Outreach
910-298-4401

Foothills Food Pantry
233 Cooper St.
Dobson, NC 27017
336-386-8405

Helping Hands of Surry County
227 Rockford St.
Mount Airy, NC 27030
336-673-0215

4. Housing and Shelters
Mount Airy Housing Authority
302 Virginia St.
Mount Airy, North Carolina
336-786-8321

The Ark (Shelter)
625 N. Bridge St.
Elkin, North Carolina
336-527-1637

5. Transportation
Mayberry Taxi
336-755-3953

Medicaid Transport
336-401-8400

Partners PKB
336-786-6155

Surry County Department
of Transportation
513 E. King St.
Dobson, NC 27017
336-386-8762

6. *Medical Services*
Surry County
Health Department
118 Hamby Rd.
Dobson, NC 27017
336-401-8400

7. *Medication*
Assistance Program
Department of Social Services
118 Hamby Rd.
Dobson, NC 27017
336-401-8700

8. *Employment/ Vocational*
Rehab/ Education
Vocational
Rehabilitation Services
784 W. Lebanon St.
Mount Airy, NC 27030
336-789-5039

9. *Legal Services*
Legal Aid-Forsyth County
102 W. 3rd St.
Winston-Salem, North Carolina
336-725-9162 or 866-472-4243

10. *Recreational/ Leisure*
Mount Airy Visitors Center
200 N. Main St.
Mount Airy, NC 27030
336-786-6116

Yadkin Valley Heritage & Trails
Visitor Center
257 Standard St.
Elkin, NC 28621
336-526-1111

11. *Special Populations*
Surry County Senior Center
215 Jones School Rd.
Mount Airy, NC 27030
336-786-6155

Surry Domestic
Violence Program
215 Jones School Rd.
Mount Airy, North Carolina
336-786-6155 (crisis)

Veteran's Service
1218 State Street
Mount Airy, NC 27030
336-783-8820 or - 8823 or
- 8824

CHAPTER 87

Swain County

1. **Mental Health and Crisis Services**
Blue Ridge Community Health Services
293 Hospital Rd., Suite C
Bryson City, NC 28713
828-477-4337

   Substance Abuse Service
   Appalachian Community Services
   100 Teptal Terrace
   Bryson City, NC 28713
   828-488-3294

   VAYA-Jackson County
   44 Bonnie Ln.
   Sylva, NC 28779
   800-849-6127

2. **Clothing/ Food Assistance/ Financial Services**
The Giving Spoon
311 Everett St.
Bryson City, North Carolina
828-488-2480

   Grace House Food Pantry
   828-497-2393

   WIC Program
   828-488-3198, extension 2002

3. **Housing and Shelters**
Qualla Housing Authority-Cherokee County
687 Acquoni Road
Cherokee, NC 28719
828-497-9161

   Salvation Army-Waynesville Corps-Haywood County
   290 Pigeon St.
   Waynesville, North Carolina
   828-456-7111

4. **Transportation**
Swain County Department of Social Services
80 Academy St.
Bryson City, NC 28713
828-488-6921

5. **Medical Services**
   Swain County
   Health Department
   545 Center St.
   Bryson City, NC 28713
   828-488-3198, extension 2002

6. **Medication**
   Assistance Program
   Swain County Family Resource
   300 Hughes Branch Rd.
   Bryson City, NC 28713
   828-488-7505

7. **Employment/ Vocational**
   Rehab/ Education
   NC Works Career Center
   101 Mitchell St.
   Bryson City, NC 28713
   828-488-2149

8. **Legal Services**
   Sylva Legal Aid-Jackson County
   1286 W. Main St.
   Sylva, North Carolina
   828-586-8931 or 800-458-6817

9. **Recreational/ Leisure**
   Swain County Visitor Center
   and Heritage Museum
   2 Everett St.
   Bryson City, NC 28713
   828-488-7857

10. **Special Populations**
    Swain County Senior Center
    125 Brendle St.
    Bryson City, NC 28713
    828-488-3047

    SAFE of Swain/Qualla
    828-488-9038 or 828-488-6809
    (Crisis Line)

CHAPTER 88

Transylvania County

1. **Mental Health and Crisis Services**
Meridian Behavioral
Health Services
69 N. Broad Street
Brevard, North Carolina
828-883-2708

Western Highlands MH/DD/
SAS, LME-Buncombe County
356 Biltmore Ave.
Asheville, North Carolina
828-225-2800

2. **Substance Abuse Services**
Blue Ridge Health
29 W. French Broad Street
Brevard, North Carolina
828-883-5550

3. **Clothing/ Food Assistance/ Financial Services**
Anchor Baptist
3232 Hendersonville Hwy.
Pisgah Forest, North Carolina
828-877-2978

God's Way Fellowship-
Food Pantry
525 Tanassee Gap Road
Balsam Grove, North Carolina
828-884-6371

NC Food Pantry
238 S. Caldwell
Brevard, NC 28712
828-877-3577

Quebec Community Center-
Food Pantry
11846 Rosman Hwy.
Lake Toxaway, North Carolina
828-862-4466

Rosman United Methodist
Church-Food Pantry
96 Church Street
Rosman, North Carolina
828-506-0062

WIC Program
828-884-3242

Zion Baptist Church-
Food Pantry
423 Main St.
Rosman, North Carolina
828-553-3478

4. **Housing and Shelters**
Brevard Housing Authority
69 W. Morgan St.
Brevard, NC 28712
828-884-2146

5. **Transportation**
Transylvania
County Transportation
828-884-3203

6. **Medical Services**
Transylvania Public
Health Department
106 E. Morgan St.
Brevard, NC 28712
828-884-3135

7. **Medication
Assistance Program**
Transylvania County
Department of Social Services
106 E. Morgan St.
Brevard, NC 28712
828-884-3174

8. **Employment/ Vocational
Rehab/ Education**
Vocational
Rehabilitation Service
203 E. Morgan St.
Brevard, North Carolina
828-833-2190

9. **Legal Services**
Legal Aid of
NC-Buncombe County
547 Haywood Rd.
Asheville, North Carolina
828-236-1080 or 877-439-3480

10. **Recreational/ Leisure**
Visitor Center Brevard &
Transylvania County
175 E. Main St.
Brevard, North Carolina
828-883-3700

11. **Special Populations**
SAFE (Domestic Violence)
828-885-7233

Silvermont Senior Center
364 E. Main St.
Brevard, NC 28712
828-884-3166

Veteran Services
844-NC4VETS

CHAPTER 89

Tyrrell County

1. **Mental Health and Crisis Services**
Tideland Mental Health/ Vidant
1208 Highway 64, East
Columbia, NC 27925
252-796-0595

2. **Substance Abuse Services**
Alcoholics Anonymous
Wesley Memorial
Methodist Church
508 Main St.
Columbia, North Carolina
252-338-1 849-4800-350-2538

   Mental Health/Substance
   Abuse Program
   Tyrell County, North Carolina
   919-946-8061

3. **Clothing/ Food Assistance/ Financial Services**
Church Road Emergency
Food Closet
Rte. 2, Box 56
Columbia, NC 27925
252-791-0916

   Food Pantry- Hyde County
   4240 Highway 264
   Scraton, NC 27875
   252-394-6461

   NC Co-op Extension
   407 Martin St.
   Columbia, NC 27925
   252-796-1581

   WIC Clinic
   252-793-1752

4. **Housing and Shelters**
IBX Hotline
Crisis Line 252-796-5526
Mideast Regional Housing
Authority-Martin County
415 East Blvd.
Williamston, NC 27889
252-789-4924

5. **Transportation**
Tyrell County Department of
Social Services
102 N. Road Street
Columbia, NC 27925
252-796-3421

Tyrell Senior Transit Program
252-793-3023

6. **Medical Services**
Columbia Medical Center
208 N. Broad Street
Columbia, NC 27925
252-796-0689

Tyrell County
Health Department
408 S. Bridge St.
Columbia, NC 27925
252-793-3023

7. **Medication
Assistance Program**
GoodRx
855-268-2822

NeedyMeds
800-503-6897

Tyrell County Department of
Social Services
102 N. Road Street
Columbia, NC 27925
252-796-3421

8. **Employment/ Vocational
Rehab/ Education**
JobLink Center
P.O. Box 449
Columbia, NC 27925
252-796-3421

NC Works Career Center-
Dare County
2522 S. Croatan Highway
Nags Head, NC 27959
252-480-3500

Vocational Rehabilitation
Services-Beaufort County
953 Washington Square Mall
Washington, NC 27889
252-946-0051

9. **Legal Services**
Legal Aid of NC
252-758-0113

Legal Services of the Coastal
Plains- Hertford County
610 Church St., East
Ahoskie, NC 27910
866-219-5262

Pamlico Sound Legal Services-
Craven County
New Bern, North Carolina
919-637-9502 or 800-672-8213

10. **Recreational/ Leisure**
Tyrell County Parks
and Recreation
108 S. Water St.
Columbia, NC 27925

Tyrell County Visitors Center
203 Ludington Dr.
Columbia, NC 27925
252-796-0723

11. Special Populations

Mobile Crisis
252-209-0388

Tyrell Senior Citizen's Center
406 Bridge St.
Columbia, NC 27925
252-796-0365 or 252-426-5753

Veterans Services
801 Main St.
Columbia, NC 27925
252-796-0000

CHAPTER 90

Union County

1. Mental Health and Crisis Services

Monarch
1653 Campus Park Dr., Unit D
Monroe, NC 28112
704-635-940

RHA Health Services
3161-B Shive Drive
Monroe, NC 28110
704-226-1517

2. Substance Abuse Services

DayMark Recovery Services
701 E. Roosevelt Blvd., #600
Monroe, NC 28112
704-296-6200

3. Clothing/ Food Assistance/ Financial Services

Open Arms Community
Outreach, Inc.
4603 Lancaster Hwy.
Monroe, NC 28112
980-269-1828

Operation Reach Out
1308 Miller St.
Monroe, NC 28110
704-289-4237

Union County Community
Shelter Food Pantry
160 Meadow St.
Monroe, NC 28110
704-261-3491

4. Housing and Shelters

Monroe Housing Authority
504 Hough Street
Monroe, North Carolina
704-289-2514

Union County Shelter
311 E. Jefferson
Monroe, North Carolina
704-289-5300

5. Transportation

Public Transit (CATS)
10006 Marvin School Rd.
Marvin, NC 28173
704-843-1680

Union County Department
of Transportation
1407 Airport Rd.
Monroe, NC 28110
704-292-2511

Union County Transportation
(Seniors)
610 Patton Ave.
Monroe, NC 28110
704-283-3713

6. **Medical Services**
Union County
Health Department
2330 Concorde Ave.
Monroe, NC 28110
704-296-4800

7. **Medication
Assistance Program**
Union County Department of
Social Services
1212 W. Roosevelt Blvd.
Monroe, North Carolina
704-296-4300

8. **Employment / Vocational
Rehab/ Education**
NC Vocational
Rehabilitation Services
1121 Skyway Dr.
Monroe, NC 28110
704-289-2543

9. **Legal Services**
Legal Services of
Southern Piedmont, Inc.-
Mecklenburg County
1431 Elizabeth Ave.
Charlotte, NC 28204
704-376-1600

Legal Aid of
NC-Cabarrus County
363 Church St., N.
Suite 200
Concord, NC 28025
704-786-4145 or 800-849-8009

10. **Recreational/ Leisure**
Visitors Center
903 Skyway Dr.
Monroe, NC 28111
704-289-4567

11. **Special Populations**
Fitzgerald Senior Center
327 S. Hayne St.
Monroe, NC 28112
704-282-4657

Senior Resource Center
1411 Dove St.
Monroe, NC 28112
704-289-9049

Union County Veterans
Services Office
407 N. Main St.
Monroe, NC 28112
704-283-3807

CHAPTER 91

Vance County

1. **Mental Health and Crisis Services**
Cardinal Innovations Healthcare
252-432-1135

Five County Mental Health, LME/ VAYA Health
134 S. Garrnett St.
Henderson, NC 27536
252-430-1330

Five County Mental Health
125 Charles Rowlands Rd.
Henderson, NC 27536 six
919-492-4011

Recovery Response Center
300 Parkview Dr., West
Henderson, NC 27536
252-438-4145

2. **Substance Abuse Services**
Addiction Recovery Center for Men
1020 County Home Rd.
Henderson, NC 27536
252-492-5746

Addiction Recovery for Women
320 Pettigrew St.
Henderson, NC 27536
252-492-5746

Genesis Substance Abuse Service
804 S. Garnett St.
Henderson, NC 27536
252-430-8774

Vance Recovery
510 Dabney Dr.
Henderson, NC 27536
252-572-2625

3. **Clothing/ Food Assistance/ Financial Services**
Harvest of Love Food Pantry
90 S. Lake Lodge Rd. Ext.
Henderson, North Carolina
252-492-1824

Meals on Wheels (Seniors)
828-233-1553

Positive Directions-The
Resource Center
336 Willow Creek Rd.
Henderson, NC 27536
252-438-2056

Salvation Army
2292 Ross Mill Rd.
Henderson, NC 27537
252-438-7101

United Way of Vance County
(Clothing)
212 Dabney Dr.
Henderson, NC 27536
252-492-8392

WIC Clinic
252-492-3147

4. Housing and Shelters
ARC for Men (Shelter)
1020 County Home Rd.
Henderson, NC 27536
252-492-5746

Catholic Charities
919-286-1964

Heart's Haven (Shelter)
516 N. Big Ford Dr.
Henderson, NC 27536
252-436-2400

Henderson House (Shelter)
169 Burwell Ave.
Henderson, NC 27536
252-430-8679

Jubilee House (Shelter)
305 S. Chestnut St.
Henderson, NC 27536
252-492-0223

Lifeline Outreach, Inc. (Shelter)
2014 Raleigh Rd.
Henderson, North Carolina
252-438-2098

Oxford House
(Recovery Shelter)
169 Burwell Ave.
Henderson, NC 27536
252-430-8679

Oxford House (Recovery)
263 Charles St.
Henderson, NC 27536
252-572-4530

Vance County
Housing Authority
224 Lincoln St.
Henderson, NC 27536
252-438-6127

5. Transportation
Kerr Area Rural Transit
Authority (KARTS)
943 W. Andrews Ave., #1
Henderson, NC 27536
252-438-2573

6. Medical Services
Maria Perham Medical Center
566 Ruin Creek Rd.
Henderson, NC 27536
252-438-4143

Vance County
Health Department
115 Charles Rowlands Rd.
Henderson, NC 27536
252-492-7915

7. **Medication Assistance Program**
Vance County Department of
Social Services
500 N. Big Ford Dr., Suite C
Henderson, NC 27536
252-492-5001

NeedyMeds
800-503-6897

8. **Employment/ Vocational Rehab/ Education**
Kittrell Job Corps
1096 US Highway 1, South
Kittrell, NC 27544
252-438-6161

Vance County Job Link
Center/ ESC
945 W. Andrews Ave., #D
Henderson, NC 27536
252-438-6129

Vocational Rehabilitation
10 Medical Ct.
Henderson, North Carolina
252-492-3141

9. **Legal Services**
Legal Aid of
NC-Durham County
201 W. Main St., Suite 400
Durham, NC 27701
919-688-6396

10. **Recreational/ Leisure**
Kerr Lake-Visitor Center (exit
214 on I -85)
946 W. Andrews Ave., #T
Henderson, NC 27536
252-438-2222 or 866-438-4565

Park Office and Visitor Center
6254 Satterwhite Pointe Rd.
Henderson, NC 27537
252-438-7791

11. **Special Populations**
AGAPE (HIV/AIDS)
903 Dorsey Ave.
Henderson, North Carolina
252-433-0364

Senior Center
500 N. Beckford Dr., Suite #D
Henderson, NC 27536
252-430-0257

VA Crisis Line (Veterans)
800-273-8255

Vance Veteran Services Officer
300 S. Garnett St., Room 115
Henderson, North Carolina
252-438-4619

CHAPTER 92

Wake County

1. ***Mental Health and Crisis Services***
Wake County Mental Health Crisis
107 Sunnybrook Rd.
Raleigh, NC 27601
919-250-1579

Wake Behavioral Health
319 Chapanoke Road, Suite 120
Raleigh, NC 27603
919-703-2845

Holly Hill Hospital
3019 Falstaff Road
Raleigh, NC 27604
919-250-7000

Crisis Line (mental health)
877-223-4617

Interact (Domestic Violence)
919-828-7740

2. ***Substance Abuse Services***
Southlight
2101 Garner Rd., Suite 107
Raleigh, NC 27610
919-832-7351

3. ***Clothing/ Food Assistance/ Financial Services***
Fuquay Emergency Food Pantry
216 W. Academy St.
Fuquay Varina, NC 27526
919-552-7720

H. O. P. E. Pantry
1809 Garner Station Boulevard
Raleigh, NC 27603
919-662-8019

FEED Ministry
1212 S. Main St., #2
Wake Forest, NC 27587
919-556-1546

Salvation Army
215 S. Person St.
Raleigh, North Carolina
919-834-6733

Shaw University
721 S. Wilmington St.
Raleigh, NC 27601
919-546-8522

4. **Housing and Shelters**
CASA
624 W. Jones St.
Raleigh, NC 27610
919-754-9960

Raleigh Housing Authority
900 Haynes Street
Raleigh, NC 27604
919-831-6416

Raleigh Rescue Mission
314 E. Hargett St.
Raleigh, NC 27601
919-828-9014 (men)
919-828-4980 (women)

Wake County
Housing Authority
100 Shannon Dr.
Zebulon, NC 27597
919-269-6404

5. **Transportation**
Go Raleigh
4104 Pool Rd.
Raleigh, NC 27610
919-485-RIDE (7433)

GO WAKE
Access Transportation
919-212-7005

Raleigh
Transportation Department
222 W. Hargett St., Suite 400
Raleigh, NC 27601
919-996-3030

6. **Medical Services**
Wake County
Health Department
10 Sunnybrook Rd.
Raleigh, NC 27610
919-250-3947

7. **Medication
Assistance Program**
Medication Assistance Program
(MAP)
101 Donald Ross Drive
Raleigh, NC 27610
919-250-3320

Wake County Department of
Social Services
220 Swinburne Rd.
Raleigh, NC 27620
919-212-7000

8. **Employment/ Vocational
Rehab/ Education**
Vocational
Rehabilitation Services
2803 Mail Service Center
Raleigh, NC 27699
919-733-7807

9. **Legal Services**
Legal Aid of North Carolina
224 S. Dawson St.
Raleigh, NC 27601
919-828-4647

10. *Recreational/ Leisure*
Carrie Park Visitor Center
215 Brookbank Hill Pl.
Cary, NC 27519
919-469-1293

Raleigh Visitor
Information Center
500 Fayetteville St.
Raleigh, NC 27601
919-834-5900

11. *Special Populations*
Diaper Bank of NC
919-886-8085

Resources for Seniors
1110 Navajo Dr., Suite 400
Raleigh, NC 27609
919-713-1556 or 919-713-1570

Services for the Blind
309 Ash Ave.
Raleigh, NC 27606
919-733-9822

Service for Deaf and Hard
of Hearing
2301 Mail Service Center
Raleigh, NC 27699
800-851-6099

Veteran Services Officer
3000 Falstaff Rd.
Raleigh, NC 27610
919-212-8387

CHAPTER 93

Warren County

1. *Mental Health and Crisis Services*
Community Corrections
132 Rafters Ln.
Warrenton, NC 27589
252-257-1309

Five County MH/ DD/ SA
548 W. Ridgeway St.
Warrenton, NC 27589
252-257-2774

Freedom House
Warrenton, North Carolina
252-879-0091

2. *Substance Abuse Services*
Al-Anon
Wesley Memorial Methodists
Warrenton, North Carolina
252-456-3404

Christ-Centered 12 Step Rec.
Ministry (Support Group)
Warrenton, North Carolina
252-257-4041

Freedom House Lake Area
(Support Group)
Norlina, North Carolina
252-456-6541

Mary Parham Hospital Rehab-
Henderson County
566 Ruin Creek Road
Henderson, NC 27536
252-436-1600 or 252-438-4143

3. *Clothing/ Food Assistance/ Financial Services*
Food Bank-Loaves and Fishes
538 W. Ridgeway St.
Warrenton, NC 27589
252-257-1160

Senior Center-Meals on Wheels
Warrenton, North Carolina
252-257-3111

United Way- Vance County
(Clothing)
715 S. Garnett St.
Henderson, NC 27536
252-492-8392

WIC Program
252-257-2116

4. **Housing and Shelters**
ARC for Men (Shelter)-
Vance County
P.O. Box 367
Henderson, NC 27536
252-492-5746

SAFE Space (Domestic
Violence)-Franklin County
800-620-6120

5. **Transportation**
Kerr Area Rural Travel
Transportation System
(KARTS)
1575 Ross Mill Rd.
Henderson, NC 27536
252-438-2573 or 800-682-4329

6. **Medical Services**
Vaya Health
800-939-5911

Warren County
Health Department
544 W. Ridgeway St.
Warrenton, NC 27589
252-257-1185

7. **Medication
Assistance Program**
NeedyMeds
800-503-6897

Warren County Department of
Social Services
307 N. Main St.
Warrenton, NC 27589
252-257-5000

8. **Employment/ Vocational
Rehab/ Education**
Franklin-Vance-Warren
Opportunity-Vance County
P.O. Box 1453
Henderson, NC 27536
252-257-1666

NC Works Career Center
210 W. Ridgeway St., Room
W-1106
Warrenton, NC 27589
252-257-3230

Vocational Rehabilitation-
Vance County
#10 Medical Court
Henderson, NC 27536
252-492-3141 or 252-598-5151

Warren County JobLink Center
309 N. Main St., Room 123
Warrenton, NC 27589
252-257-3230

Warren County
Workforce Center
309 N. Main St.
Warrenton, NC 27589
252-257-3230

9. **Legal Services**
   Legal Aid of
   NC-Durham County
   201 W. Main St., Suite 400
   Durham, NC 27701
   919-688-6396 or 800-331-7594

   NC Bar Association
   Referral Line
   800-662-7660

10. **Recreational/ Leisure**
    Warren County Community
    Center, Inc.
    111 W. Franklin St.
    Warrenton, NC 27589
    252-257-3407

    Warren County Department of
    Parks and Recreation
    113 Wilcox St.
    Warrenton, NC 27589
    252-257-2272

11. **Special Populations**
    Veteran Services Officer
    309 N. Main St.
    Warrenton, NC 27589
    252-257-3385

    Warren County Senior Center
    Warrenton, North Carolina
    252-257-3111

    Warren County
    Veterans Services
    Courthouse
    109 S. Main St.
    Warrenton, NC 27589
    252-257-3360

CHAPTER 94

Washington County

1. ***Mental Health and Crisis Services***
Albemarle MHC/SAS/DD
716 Washington St.
Plymouth, NC 27962
252-793-1154

   DREAM Provider Care Services
716 Washington St.
Plymouth, NC 27962
252-791-0430 or 877-282-0837

   Vidant Behavioral Health
804 Washington St.
Plymouth, NC 27962

2. ***Substance Abuse Services***
DREAM Provider Care Services
703 N. Broad Street
Edenton, NC 27962
252-946-0585

   Mental Health/Substance
Abuse Program
Washington County,
North Carolina
252-793-1154

3. ***Clothing/ Food Assistance/ Financial Services***
Economic Improvement
Council, Inc.-Chowan County
712 Virginia Rd.
Edenton, NC 27932
252-482-4495

   Food Pantry of
Washington County
811 Washington St.
Plymouth, North Carolina
252-793-4152

   Roper Methodists Church
8001 NC-32
Roper, NC 27970
252-797-7503

   WIC Clinic
252-791-3116

4. **Housing and Shelters**
Catholic Charities
252-426-7717

Cross Coalition LTD
101 Virginia Pine Dr.
Plymouth, NC 27962
252-809-2355

New Life CDC Plymouth
Plymouth, NC 27962
252-791-0095

Option to Domestic Violence
(Women Shelter)
211 Washington St.
Plymouth, NC 27962
252-793-9514 or 252-940-1046

Plymouth Housing Authority
306 W. Water St.
Plymouth, NC 27962
252-793-3188

5. **Transportation**
Riverlight
Public Transportation
209 E. Main St.
Plymouth, NC 27962
252-793-4041

6. **Medical Services**
Martin-Tyrell-Washington
Dental Health Clinic
198 NC Highway 45, North
Plymouth, NC 27962
252-793-1851

Washington County
Health Department
198 NC Highway 45, North
Plymouth, NC 27962
252-793-3023

Washington County Hospital
958 US 64, East
Plymouth, North Carolina
252-793-4135

7. **Medication Assistance Program**
Good Rx
855-268-2822

Needy Meds
800-503-6897

Rx Outreach
PO Box 66536
St. Louis, MO 63166
888-796-1234

Washington County
Department of Social Services
209 E. Main St.
Plymouth, NC 27962
252-793-4041 or 252-975-5500

8. **Employment/ Vocational Rehab/ Education**
JobLink Center/ ESC
P.O. Box 10
Plymouth, NC 27962
252-793-4041

Vocational
Rehabilitation Services
814 Washington Sq., Mall
Plymouth, NC 27889
252-946-0051

9. **Legal Services**
   Legal Aid of
   NC-Hertford County
   610 Church St., East
   Ahoskie, NC 27910
   252-758-0113 or 866-219-5262

   Pamlico Sound Legal Services-
   Craven County
   New Bern, North Carolina
   919-637-9502 or 800-672-8213

10. **Recreational/ Leisure**
   Tourism and Visitor's Center
   701 Washington St.
   Plymouth, North Carolina
   252-793-3248 or 252-793-4801

   Washington County Parks
   and Recreation
   603 Adams St.
   Plymouth, NC 27962
   252-793-6607

11. **Special Populations**
   IBX Hotline
   (Crisis Intervention)
   252-796-5526

   Veterans Services
   112 Latham Ave., #1
   Plymouth, NC 27962
   252-793-3197

   Washington County Senior
   Citizens Center
   198 NC Highway 45, North
   Plymouth, NC 27962
   252-793-3816

CHAPTER 95

Watauga County

1. **Mental Health and Crisis Services**
DayMark Recovery Services
132 Popular Grove Connector, Suite B
Boone, NC 28607
828-264-8759

2. **Substance Abuse Services**
New River Behavioral
Healthcare-Watauga County
895 State Farm Road, Suite 508
Boone, NC 28607
828-264-9007

New River Serenity (Recovery for Men)
8043 US 221
Boone, North Carolina
828-262-1542

3. **Clothing/ Food Assistance/ Financial Services**
Hunger and Health Coalition
141 Health Center Dr., Suite C
Boone, NC 28607
828-262-1628

WIC Program
919-707-5800

4. **Housing and Shelters**
Northwestern
Regional Housing
869 Highway 105, Extension
Suite 7
Boone, NC 28607
828-266 9794

Hospitality House (Shelter)
302 King St.
Boone, North Carolina
828-264-1237

5. **Transportation**
Appalcart
305 NC Highway 105, Bypass
Boone, NC 28607
828-297-1300

Senior Transportation
814 W. King St.
Boone, NC 28607
828-265-8090

6. **Medical Services**
Watauga County
Health Department
126 Poplar Grove Connector
Boone, North Carolina
828-264-4995

7. **Medication
Assistance Program**
Watauga County Department
of Social Services
132 Poplar Grove Connector,
Suite C
Boone, NC 28607
828-265-8100

8. **Employment/ Vocational
Rehab/ Education**
Vocational
Rehabilitation Service
245 Winkler's Creek Road, #A
Boone, NC 28607
828-265-5396

9. **Legal Services**
Legal Aid
171 Grand Blvd.
Boone, North Carolina
828-264-5640 or 800-849-5666

10. **Recreational/ Leisure**
Boone Area Visitor Center
331 Queen St., Suite 101
Boone, North Carolina
828-266-1345

11. **Special Populations**
Cove Creek Community
1081 Old Highway 421
Sugar Grove, North Carolina
828-297-5195
Oasis, Inc. (Domestic Violence)
Crisis Line – 828-262-5035

Senior Center
132 Poplar Grove Connector,
Suite A
Boone, North Carolina
828-265-8090

Veteran Services
126 Poplar Grove Connector
Rooms 206 & 207
Boone, NC 28607
828-265-8065

CHAPTER 96

Wayne County

1. **Mental Health and Crisis Services**
Eastpointe Human Services
100 S. James St.
Goldsboro, North Carolina
800-913-6109

Family Works
Psychological Services
1410 E. Ash St.
Goldsboro, NC 27530
910-509-0588

Mental Health Association of
Wayne County
1608 E. Pine St.
Goldsboro, NC 27530
919-734-6676

Wayne County Mental
Health Association
719 E. Ash St.
Goldsboro, NC 27530
919-734-3530

Waynesboro Family Clinic
1706 Wayne Memorial Dr.
Goldsboro, NC 27534
919-734-6676

2. **Substance Abuse Services**
AA
919-735-4221

Potter's Wheel Ministries (6
months program)
147 Faith Ln.
Mount Olive, North Carolina
919-658-3534

Narcotics Anonymous
St. Paul United
Methodist Church
Goldsboro, NC 27530
919-734-2965

3. **Clothing/ Food Assistance/ Financial Services**
American Red Cross
600 N. George St.
Goldsboro, NC 27530
919-735-7201

Community Soup Kitchen
112 W. Oak St.
Goldsboro, NC 27530
919-731-3939

Harvest Fellowship Church
126 W. Walnut St.
Goldsboro, NC 27530
919-922-4107

Meals on Wheels (Seniors)
601 Royall Ave.
Goldsboro, North Carolina
919-734-1178

Salvation Army (Clothing)
610 N. William St.
Goldsboro, NC 27530
919-735-4811, extension 100

United Church Ministries of
Wayne County, Inc.
119 W. Walnut St.
Goldsboro, NC 27530
919-734-0480

WIC Clinic
919-731-1276

4. *Housing and Shelters*
Catholic Charities
919-947-0802

City Mission (Shelter)
304 E. Mulbery St.
Goldsboro, North Carolina
919-731-4530

Eastern Carolina Regional
Housing Authority
2120 S. Slocumb Street
Goldsboro, North Carolina
919-735-0435

Flynn House (Recovery)
409 N. George St.
Goldsboro, North Carolina
919-734-1718

Goldsboro Housing Authority
1729 Edgerton
Goldsboro, North Carolina
919-735-5650 or 919-735-4226

House of Fordham
412 N. William St.
Goldsboro, North Carolina
919-736-7352

Mount Olive
Housing Authority
108 W. Main St.
Mount Olive, North Carolina
919-658-6682

Oxford House (Recovery Men)
1300 E. Ash St.
Goldsboro, North Carolina
919-583-8441

Oxford House
(Recovery Women)
1008 E. Walnut St.
Goldsboro, North Carolina
919-735-1241

5. **Transportation**
GATEWAY Transit
Goldsboro-Wayne
Transportation Authority
600 N. Madison Ave.
Goldsboro, North Carolina
919-736-1374

Wayne County
DSS Transportation
301 N. Herman St.
Goldsboro, North Carolina
919-580-4034

6. **Medical Services**
Goshen/Rosewood
Dental Services
104 Adair Drive, #C
Goldsboro, NC 27530
919-648-4437

Wayne County
Health Department
301 N. Herman St., Box CC
Goldsboro, NC 27530
919-731-1000 or 919-731-1302

7. **Medication
Assistance Program**
Community Crisis Center
607 S. Slocumb St.
Goldsboro, NC 27530
919-734-6836

Wayne County Department of
Social Services
301 N. Herman St., Box HH
Goldsboro, NC 27530
919-580-4034

8. **Employment/ Vocational
Rehab/ Education**
NC Works Career Center/Job
Link Center
2006 Wayne Memorial Dr.
Goldsboro, NC 27534
919-731-7950

Vocational Rehabilitation
2719 Graves Dr., Suite 14
Goldsboro, NC 27534
919-778-3795

9. **Legal Services**
Legal Aid-Wilson County
866-219-5262

Legal Services of Eastern
North Carolina
1025 S. William St.
Goldsboro, NC 27530
919-731-2303

10. **Recreational/ Leisure**
Boys and Girls Clubs of
Wayne County
1401 Royall Ave.
Goldsboro, NC 27534
919-735-2358

Family Y
1105 Parkway Drive
Goldsboro, NC 27532
919-778-8557

Seymour Johnson Air Force
Base Visitor Center
1050 Wright Brothers Ave.
Seymour Johnson AFB,
NC 27531
919-722-1343

Wayne County Parks
and Recreation
901 E. Ash St.
Goldsboro, NC 27530
919-739-7480

Wayne County Visitors Center
801 US 117, South
Goldsboro, NC 27530
919-731-1653

11. *Special Populations*
Senior Center/Wayne County
Services for Aging
2001 E. Ash St.
Goldsboro, NC 27530
919-731-1591

Wayne County Veterans
Service Office
2001 E. Ash St., #D
Goldsboro, NC 27530
919-731-1490

Wayne Uplift Domestic
Violence and Sexual
Assault Program
719 E. Ash St.
Goldsboro, North Carolina
919-736-1313

CHAPTER 97

Wilkes County

1. **Mental Health and Crisis Services**
CareNet Counseling
110 Jefferson St., Suite 106
North Wilkesboro, NC 28659
336-838-1644

DayMark Recovery Services-
Wilkes County
1400 Willow Ln.
West Park C61-2
North Wilkesboro, NC 28659
336-667-5151

Synergy Recovery
118 Peace St.
North Wilkesboro, NC 28659
336-667-7191, extension 228
Crisis Line-866-275-9552

2. **Substance Abuse Services**
Smokey Mountain Center
800-849-6127

VAYA Health
723 Main St.
Wilkesboro, NC 28659
800 849-6127

3. **Clothing/ Food Assistance/ Financial Services**
Meals on Wheels
710 Veterans Dr.
North Wilkesboro, NC 28659
336-667-7174

Samaritan Kitchen of Wilkes
4187 US-421
Wilkesboro, NC 28697
336-838-5331

4. **Housing and Shelters**
Northwestern Regional
Housing Authority
215 W. South St.
Wilkesboro, NC 28697
336-667-8979

North Wilkesboro
Housing Authority
101 Hickory St.
North Wilkesboro, NC 28659
336-667-3203

5. *Transportation*
Wilkes County Transit
Authority (WTA)
1010 Spring St.
Wilkesboro, NC 28697
336-838-1272

6. *Medical Services*
Wilkes County
Health Department
306 College St.
Wilkesboro, NC 28697
336-651-7450

7. *Medication*
Assistance Program
Wilkes County Department of
Social Services
304 College St.
Wilkesboro, NC 28697
336-651-7400

8. *Employment/ Vocational*
Rehab/ Education
Vocational
Rehabilitation Services
318 Wilkesboro Ave.
Wilkesboro, North Carolina
336-667-1205

9. *Legal Services*
High Country Legal Aid-
Watauga County
171 Grand Blvd.
Boone, NC 28607
828-355-4890

10. *Recreational/ Leisure*
Northwest NC Visitor Center
2121 E. US Highway 421
North Wilkesboro, NC 28659
336-667-1259

11. *Special Populations*
SAFE Inc.
336-838-7233

Suicide Prevention
800-273-8255

Veteran Services
416 Executive Dr.
Wilkesboro, NC 28697
336-651-7327

Wilkes Senior Center
228 Fairplans School Rd.
North Wilkesboro, NC 28659
336-667-5281

CHAPTER 98

Wilson County

1. **Mental Health and Crisis Services**
Mental Health Association
509 W. Nash St.
Wilson, NC 27894
252-243-2773

Mental Health/Substance
Abuse Program
Wilson County, North Carolina
252-399-8021

Wilson-Greene Mental
Health Center
1709 S. Tarboro St.
Wilson, North Carolina
252-243-3499

2. **Substance Abuse Services**
PORT Human Services-
Pitt County
4300 Sapphire Ct., #110
Greenville, North Carolina
252-830-7540

Walter B. Jones, ADATC-
Pitt County
2577 W. 5th St.
Greenville, NC 27834
252-830-3426

Wilson Crisis Center
252-237-5156

3. **Clothing/ Food Assistance/ Financial Services**
Emergency Assistance Program
First Baptist Church
311 W. Nash St.
Wilson, NC 27893
252-243-5163

Harvest Christian Fellowship-
Food Distribution
307 W. Spring St.
Lucama, NC 27851

Lebanon United Methodist
Church-Food Pantry
7224 Lindell Rd.
Statonsburg, NC 27883
252-238-2717

Living Faith Church-Food
Distribution Center
3338 Corbett Ave.
Elm City, NC 27822
252-291-1573

Meals on Wheels
2306 Cedar Run Pl., NW
Wilson, North Carolina
252-237-1303

Salvation Army
316 W. Tarboro St.
Wilson, North Carolina
252-243-2696

Soup Kitchen
P.O. Box 1527
Wilson, NC 27894
252-243-6208

WIC Clinic
252-291-3144, extension 6650

4. **Housing and Shelters**
Hope Station (Men)
309 Goldsboro St., East
Wilson, NC 27893
252-291-7278

Wesley Shelter (Domestic
Violence)/Transitions
Homeless Shelter
106 E. Vance St.
Wilson, North Carolina
252-291-2344

5. **Transportation**
Wilson County Transportation
2201 Miller Rd., South
Wilson, NC 27893
252-399-2817

Wilson Transit System
320 E. Nash St.
Wilson, NC 27893
252-399-2488

6. **Medical Services**
Wilson Community
Health Center
303 E. Greene St.
Wilson, NC 27893
252-243-9800

Wilson County
Health Department
1801 Glendale Dr., SW
Wilson, NC 27893
252-237-3141

7. **Medication
Assistance Program**
Love in Action
113 S. Tarboro St.
Wilson, NC 27893
252-291-9880

Wilson County Department of
Social Services
100 Gold St., NW
Wilson, NC 27894
252-406-4000

8. *Employment/ Vocational Rehab/ Education*
N.C. Works Career Center
302 Tarboro St., West
Wilson, NC 27893
252-234-1129

Vocational Rehabilitation
306 W. Nash St.
Wilson, NC 27893
252-237-7161

9. *Legal Services*
Legal Aid of NC
208 N. Goldsboro St.
Wilson, NC 27893
252-291-6851 or 800-682-7902

10. *Recreational/ Leisure*
Wilson Parks and
Recreation Department
1800 Herring Ave.
Wilson, NC 27893
252-399-2261

Wilson Visitors Center
301 Goldsboro St., South
Wilson, NC 27893
252-243-8440

YMCA
3436 Airport Blvd.
Wilson, NC 27896
252-291-9622

11. *Special Populations*
Telamon Corporation
(Services for Migrant and
Seasonal Workers)
302 W. Tarboro St.
Wilson, NC 27893
252-291-1203

Wilson County Office of
Senior Affairs
252-237-1303

Wilson County Senior Center
1808 S. Goldsboro St.
Wilson, North Carolina
252-291-1203

Veteran Services
1901 S. Tarboro St.
Wilson, North Carolina
252-237-2422

CHAPTER 99

Yadkin County

1. **Mental Health and Crisis Services**

Crossroads Healthcare, LME-Surry County
200 Elkin Business Park Dr.
Elkin, NC 28621
336-835-1000 or 888-235-4671

Mental Health/Substance Abuse Program
336-725-8389

Jodi Province Counseling Services, PLLC
714-A Carolina Avenue
Yadkinville, NC 27055
336-818-0733

2. **Substance Abuse Services**

Alpha Acres
1939 Morningstar Drive
Yadkinville, NC 27055
336-463-5155

DayMark Recovery Services
320 E. Lee Ave.
Yadkinville, NC 27055
336-679-8805

New Dawn Recovery Program
624 W. Main St.
Yadkinville, NC 27055
336-679-6718

3. **Clothing/ Food Assistance/ Financial Services**

Goodwill (Clothing)
917 S. State Street
Yadkinville, NC 27055
336-679-2040

Meals on Wheels
336-367-3522

Union Grove Baptist Church-Food Pantry
2401 Nebo Road
Yadkinville, North Carolina
336-961-5792

United Way
127-D W. Main St.
Yadkinville, NC 27055
336-679-4462

WIC Clinic
336-849-7910

Yadkin Christian Ministries
(Emergency Food)
121 W. Elm St.
Yadkinville, NC 27055
336-677-3080

4. **Housing and Shelters**
Giving Hand Foundation
431Wyo Road
Yadkinville, NC 27055
336-463-2073

The Ark Homeless Shelter-
Surry County
130 Hill St.
Elkin, NC 28621
336-527-1637

Tri-County Christian
Crisis Ministry
440 W. Main St.
Jonesville, NC 28642
336-526-1089

United Way
336-679-4462

Yadkin Valley Economic
Development District
(Housing Assistance)
533 N. Carolina Ave.
Boonville, NC 27011
336-367-7251 or 336-679-2071

5. **Transportation**
Community Action Program
533 N. Carolina Ave.
Boonville, NC 27011
336-367-7251

PART BUS
800-588-7787

YVEDDI
Boonville, North Carolina
336-367-7175 or 336-463-4137

Yadkin Valley
Public Transportation
533 N. Carolina Ave.'s
Highway 601, North
Boonville, NC 27011
336-367-3520

6. **Medical Services**
Yadkin County
Health Department
320 W. Maple St.
Yadkinville, NC 27055
336-679-4203 or 336-349-7910

7. **Medication
Assistance Program**
Yadkin County Department of
Social Services
250 Willow Street
Yadkinville, NC 27055
336-849-7910 or 336-679-4210

Good Rx
855-268-2822

Needy Meds
800-503-6897

Rx Outreach
P.O. Box 66536
St. Louis, MO 63166
888-796-1234

8. **Employment/ Vocational Rehab/ Education**

Employment
Security Commission
106 E. Elm St.
Yadkinville, NC 27055
336-679-4079

JobLink Center
233 E. Main St.
Yadkinville, NC 27055
336-312-9960 or 336-679-7833

9. **Legal Services**

Legal Aid-Forsyth County
102 W. 3rd St., Suite 460
Winston-Salem, NC 27101
336-75-9162 or 866-472-4243

10. **Recreational/ Leisure**

Jonesville Welcome Center
1503 NC Highway 67
Jonesville, NC 28642

Yadkin Tourism and
Development Authority
205 S. Jackson St.
Yadkinville, NC 27055
877-492-3546

Yadkin Valley Heritage
and Trails Visitor Center-
Surry County
257 Standard St.
Elkin, NC 28621
336-526-1111

11. **Special Populations**

East Bend Senior Center
473 E. Main St.
East Bend, NC 27018
336-699-5100

Veterans Services
101 S. State Street
Yadkinville, NC 27055
336-679-8209

Yadkin County Senior Center
207 E. Hemlock St.
Yadkinville, NC 27055
336-679-3596, extension 562

Yadkin Domestic Violence
336-679-2500

CHAPTER 100

Yancey County

1. **Mental Health and Crisis Services**
RHA Health Services-West
72 Blue Ridge Ln.
Burnsville, North Carolina
828-682-2111

2. **Substance Abuse Services**
VAYA Health
72 Blue Ridge Ln.
Burnsville, NC 28714
800-849-6127

3. **Clothing/ Food Assistance/ Financial Services**
Green Mountain Presbyterian
Church-Food Pantry
299 Toe River Rd.
Green Mountain, NC 28740

Reconciliation House
20 Academy St.
Burnsville, North Carolina
828-682-7251

The Full Gospel Food Pantry
South Toe Old
Presbyterian Church
5400 NC Highway 80, South
Burnsville, NC 28714
828-284-0375

WIC Program-Toe River
Health District
202 Medical Campus Dr.
Burnsville, North Carolina
828-682-6118

4. **Housing and Shelters**
Housing Authority-
Northwestern Regional
23 Woodland Dr.
Burnsville, North Carolina
828-682-2216

5. **Transportation**
Yancey County
Transportation Authority
115 Mitchell Branch Rd.
Burnsville, North Carolina
828-682-6144

6. **Medical Services**
Yancey County
Health Department
202 Medical Campus Dr.
Burnsville, NC 28714
828-682-6118

7. **Medication Assistance Program**
Yancey County Department of
Social Services
320 Pensacola Rd.
Burnsville, NC 28714
828-682-6148

8. **Employment/ Vocational Rehab/ Education**
NC Works Career Center
1040 E. US Highway 19 E.
Burnsville, North Carolina
828-682-6618

Work First
828-682-2470

9. **Legal Services**
Pisgah Legal Services-
Buncombe County
89 Montford Ave.
Asheville, NC 28801
828-253-0406

10. **Recreational/ Leisure**
Burnsville-Yancey
Visitor Center
106 W. Main St.
Burnsville, NC 28714

11. **Special Populations**
Family Violence Coalition of
Yancey County
Crisis Line (Domestic Violence)
828-682-0056

Veteran Services
110 Town Square
Burnsville, North Carolina
828-682-1514

Yancey County Senior Center
503 Medical Campus Dr.
Burnsville, North Carolina
828-682-0611

APPENDIX I:

MAP OF NORTH CAROLINA, USA (COUNTIES)

www.gisgeography.com